LANGUAGE OF THE HEART: UNCONDITIONAL LOVE

LIVING FULLY EMPOWERED

LAURIE MARTIN

Copyright © 2014 by Laurie Martin

All rights reserved. No part of this publication may be reproduced, stored in a retrieval system, or transmitted in any form or by any means, electronic, mechanical, photocopy, recording, or otherwise, without prior written permission from Laurie Martin, with the exception of short excerpts used with acknowledgement of the author.

ISBN-10: 0986020141
ISBN-13: 9780986020148
Library of Congress Control Number: 2014909947
Mindful Meetings, Naples, FL

Praise for

LANGUAGE OF THE HEART: UNCONDITIONAL LOVE, LIVING FULLY EMPOWERED

"Language of the Heart: Unconditional Love is a GREAT book! It gives you the tools and step-by-step information to have a spiritually strong relationship with yourself. I enjoyed reading every page. I think it is just as informative as any of Wayne Dyer's books."

—Carroll Johnson-Welsh, Librarian

"It is abundantly clear in Laurie's writing that she speaks authentically from her heart. She presents practical and actionable advice to the reader on how to live a more love-based existence. This book gives the reader alternative methods to reframe his or her thought processes. Laurie's text helps us challenge the mundane and appreciate the full potential each of us has available in our everyday life."

—Dr. John Papandrea, Marriage and Family Therapist

"Laurie Martin delivers a powerful book that not only improves your communication skills, it changes the way you interact with yourself and others from the standpoint of divinity, love, confidence, and peace. The skills you will gain from reading this book are priceless. Language of the Heart: Unconditional Love is unconditional in itself by offering a genuine read into Laurie's life and it serves as the catalyst we all need in order to look into our own life. It's a must read for people of all ages, demographics, and backgrounds."

–David Mezzapelle, bestselling author of the
Contagious Optimism book series

"I love this book! It taught me how to live outside the box. As I read it, my whole vibration changed, it's so empowering. It gave me a deeper understanding about unconditional love and provided helpful uplifting perspectives to manage my thoughts, emotions and beliefs. I really appreciate the effective communication skills, and numerous exercises and visualization techniques. I highly recommend it!"

–Carol Natalotto, Owner of CEL Management Pty Ltd

"The more I read Language of the Heart: Unconditional Love, I felt a weight lift off of my shoulders. All of my worries and attachments started making sense and I didn't see them as burdens any longer. I saw them as an opportunity to grow, accept and love myself more. Laurie's writing style makes the concepts and ideas easy to relate to and understand!"

–Astrid Martinez WBTV/CBS Reporter/Anchor

"The mind and emotion can dictate your entire health, and Laurie Martin does a fantastic job of teaching how to heal on the deeper emotional levels. She writes about this extremely difficult level of healing to make it simple, concise and functional to any reader."

-Dr. Lindsay Thomas, Chiropractor

CONTENTS

Chapter 1	Unconditional Love for Self: Our Most Natural State	1
Chapter 2	Observing Attachments and Processing Emotions	23
Chapter 3	Unconditional Acceptance and Forgiveness: No More Judgment	73
Chapter 4	Evolving and Expanding Your Awareness Rapidly	105
Chapter 5	Effective Communication Skills	123
Chapter 6	Stepping into Your Sovereignty: The Authentic You	149
About the Author		171

DEDICATION

To my mom,
I love you and miss you. Thank you for being my mom.
I look forward to seeing again some day!

APPRECIATION

There are so many people to thank. I want to give a heartfelt thank-you to all my family and friends who walk beside me in friendship, support me on my path, love me, help me, and encourage me with kindness! You have blessed my life immeasurably! I'm also extremely grateful to all the speakers and authors who have shared information that supported me, empowered and inspired me throughout my life! And a big thank you to the unseen loving help from above that helps not only me but all of you, too.

Thank you so much to my professional support:

Cover design by Kerry Fischel, Editing by Michael Carr

PR by Cindy Dobyns, Abovewater.com, Terri Rose-Anderson of

VisionServer, and the Photo by Charlie McDonald

INTRODUCTION

My journey of self-growth has involved not just one specific technique for each occurrence of getting back to inner peace. Rather, it has been an amalgamation of information that I was ready to awaken to, which was directly aligned with *who I was at the time*. Each of us draws the exact information to us that we are meant to have, precisely when we need it, and it happens through our own intention. A resonance with something or someone is about a vibrational match. You may notice that you have been drawn to specific wisdom from someone, or a specific tool, and as you evolved you were drawn to new information and new tools that worked for you in that moment. As we evolve so do our tools.

A major theme of mine in the past has been to deepen my trust in all areas of my life: trust in my intuitive abilities, my manifesting abilities, myself as a sovereign being, my ability to bring my body and mind into balance—and my trust that all is well. I have learned so much during this time! In this book, I have included tools that I've learned from others along my life's journey, as well as stories, my own insights, and many tools I discovered during my own self-healing. The tools help us process our emotions. It's not about just focusing on positive thoughts and language. Imagine a garbage can filled to the rim with junk food. The junk food represents your subconscious mind, which stores your past hurts, disappointments, attachments, fears, anger, worries, *and your beliefs*. The subconscious mind is similar to a tape recorder. It records every thought, belief, and perceived experience and creates programs in the body. The healthy food represents the affirmations. Now imagine someone trying to shove healthy food into an already full garbage bin. There's no room, because the garbage is still there. It's the same with our emotions. We need to process our hurts, anger, disappointments, fears, and jealousies. We can't ignore them. They have a specific energetic vibration. The energy vibration of fear, anger, suffering, hatred and anxiety emit a much different vibrational output than those emotions of love, joy, and gratitude. As a result, they attract a different frequency, hence outcome. Electromagnetic energy fields surround all living organisms. These energy fields are inside and outside of us. This means that on the microscopic level, every system, organ, tissue, cell, and molecule of the human body has its own field of electromagnetic vibrational energy. This subtle energy system is in the infrastructure of all of us. Everything is energy exchange. This is why it is so important to spend time daily to process our emotions.

A technique that I highly recommend is *meridian tapping*, which helps harmonize the body. By tapping on specific acupuncture points and using specific language, you can bring the body back to a balanced state. You can research meridian tapping on the Internet. There are several different methods.

At the end of chapter 2, I include an exercise called "Processing Your Emotions," which you can use daily. Processing your worries, fears, and sadness is an action of self-love. You have the power to interrupt your negative patterning and train your brain and body to think differently. You have the power to *draw your energy back* to love and trust. You have the power to direct your life in a way that is aligned with your highest good. In other words, you have the power to create your own reality. Trust your emotions and your intuition. They are guiding you. You are being guided, and love is calling you!

Throughout this book, I use the term "the Divine." Please feel free to replace it with whatever word resonates best for you in conveying pure and complete positive vibration and the source of unconditional love.

Each of us has chosen specific aspects to learn and experience here during our life on earth. From my late twenties on, this was the beginning of my awareness of my life theme of learning about self-love and empowerment. I had three radical changes at one time: my boyfriend and I broke up, my grandfather passed away, and I was fired from a job. Feeling like a failure, lost, alone, and rejected, I picked up my first self-help book. My thirst for spiritual knowledge began from this point. I can even remember looking at a quiz in a magazine, titled "How spiritual are you?" I didn't even know what that *meant*. I became fascinated with such questions as *why are we here on earth? Is there life somewhere else? Who am I? What is intuition?* I read every book I could find on near-death experiences because I was intrigued with what heaven was like, and wanted to make sense of all the loving messages that resonated with me. I attended numerous inspirational, spiritual, healing, and motivational workshops.

The more we take responsibility for our energy, the more we awaken. I've come to understand that it's never about blaming someone outside myself for *my* strong emotions. I love getting to the awareness of discovering just what belief, attachment, insecurity, or fear is not in congruence with my full empowerment. What, exactly, is *behind* the emotion that got triggered in me? In many of these major discoveries, I have strengthened my sense of self. And I am impassioned to pass on my wisdom and knowledge for others to help themselves. And my intention is for you to feel your own love, greatness, and divinity!

If you are reading this book, then you're interested in expanding and integrating into more of your own light. We are claiming our sovereignty and walking back to our remembrance of who we are: divine, infinite, radiant, powerful beings. As energetic beings, we are connected to the oneness of everything. You are much more powerful than you believe. You are very much needed in the entire orchestration of the cosmos. I believe that before each of us became a human being, a singular construct, we were spirits of light and consciousness having experiences in other dimensions, with full memory of our beautiful, divine selves. Now we are evolving back to this remembrance here on earth. And the path I have learned is through love. The path to self-love is ongoing. At times, we think we have learned something, and then we find that "here we are again."

Relationships with others help us see how we play the game of life. People on a path of personal growth are identifying their emotional attachment and inner charge, observing their behavior, moving out of the blame game and taking responsibility. As you continue reading, enjoy the language of your own heart. **Language of the Heart: Unconditional Love** is infused with the intention that you feel uplifted and inspired while reading it. May it be a spark that touches your soul, walks you into your heart and helps set you free!

UNCONDITIONAL LOVE FOR SELF: OUR MOST NATURAL STATE

Unconditional love is one of the most important things to learn about on our self-growth journey. Unconditional love is who we are and who created us. It is our most natural and organic state of being. This is why millions of people are being spiritually pulled to remember who they are and to love themselves. A state of unconditional love brings us back to a state of freedom, harmony and empowerment. When we are not in this state it is unnatural, maybe even uncomfortable, because it is not our highest and most powerful state of being. To connect with unconditional love, we need to explore our connection to our inner self and be at peace with who we are. As we all become more peaceful within, we create a ripple effect that is felt by many.

This doesn't mean we are going to live 100 percent of our life here on earth in a space of unconditional love. What it does mean is that we have a desire to grow into living in a space of love, joy and peace. When we are spinning in the slipstream of fear or anxiousness we have the power to catch ourselves and instantly draw our energy back to ourselves. Does that make sense? It means that we hold the energy of living and being unconditional love, knowing that it's the material that is within every part of us. And this honors the Divine and our own DNA. It's an indication that we value all life. If we are love, then by fueling ourselves up with love, we are coding our system with the highest octane. It's like using high-test instead of regular gasoline; it's like eating a spinach and kale salad with sunflower sprouts instead of a deep-fried chili-cheese steak sandwich on white bread. Why not fuel yourself with the highest life-sustaining thoughts and energy? Why not remember that you are *whole*? Why not trust your life path? But wait—what does that even mean? It means that the beautiful, infinite, powerful being that you are right now is a divine formula and essence of love and light—an aspect of the Divine. You were perfectly designed without missing any parts or needing anything to validate your worthiness. Turn to the light within you and trust it, appreciate it, love it, connect with it, and respect it. Being fearful is not honoring your light unless it's for your physical safety. A feeling of safety and worthiness comes from *within*—it is independent of any other person.

    Each soul signed up for this earth life for the experience and growth in consciousness. You are on the path that you signed up for. As you grow into your light you naturally help others do it, too. Each person lives in a reality that she or he chooses to experience. And there is no "better than" or "less than"; it's about having an *experience*. You are always right where you were meant to be. As we evolve our consciousness we raise our vibration. The more we process our fears and anchor in unconditional love both within ourselves and from the Divine, and the more we embody this love, the more we help increase the earth's vibration and raise the consciousness of the entire planet. A higher consciousness means more inner peace, freedom, ease, well-being, and lightness, because we stay connected to our intuition, the Divine, and grounded in a state of neutrality.

Many of us have not been taught how to live in an unconditionally loving way toward ourselves, which is the most powerful and authentic way to be. We were taught to get an education; work; achieve; respect the boss, parents, and teachers; marry and raise a family. We gave much of our power and authority to external things. Now, we are being supported and guided to learn about the importance of inner peace, unconditional love, fulfillment, trusting self, and trusting our intuition. We learn how to cultivate inner beauty by practicing appreciating and supporting our needs and desires. This is the foundation of self-love. Many of us are being internally led to move into empowerment, into love and light moving towards equality. We are learning to trust ourselves in a way that really understands our inner light and capabilities of being an evolved spiritual being in human form on earth.

In meditation, I asked, *if this is our most natural and intrinsic state, how can I use unconditional love as my inspiration to guide me?* I began examining those occasions when I was being conditional with myself and others, and learning why this was happening. The *why* helped me identify my insecurity, attachments, expectations, and fears. And I began asking, *what am I looking for or needing? What am I attached to?* And *how can I expand my love?*

My dogs have been my greatest teachers of unconditional love. On our daily walks, they're 100 percent in the moment. They are eager to meet new people. They have big smiles on their faces and are filled with excitement and joy as they run up to new people with pure love. They are not fearful that people are not going to like them; they are not afraid of rejection. They are not criticizing or judging others for how they look. They don't have attachments or conditions. They are pure, unconditional love. They jump around, always happy to see everyone. When I look at my dogs, they teach me to be in my heart. So I asked myself, *why am I not as happy and excited as my dogs are to see every new human being who walks past me?* What I uncovered was this: I was afraid of being judged.

Many of us have some fear of rejection. Our job is to keep our heart pure—be a pure heart and express a pure heart—not to cover it up out of fear of getting hurt. Our natural state is to be vulnerable and be seen. It's time to own your beautiful soul signature and shine bright! Your soul signature is as unique as your fingerprints. No one has your soul signature. And your unique puzzle piece is needed for the completion of the universal whole. It contains everything about you: the full essence of who you are, your experiences, your beliefs, your perceptions, and your pure light.

In another meditation, I had the image of seeing a beautiful, huge diamond the size of a lightbulb. The diamond had little crevices of dirt left in its surface. The remaining dirt represented the last tendrils of self-doubt. The message was simple: the more I trust, the more I shine. And I pass this message onto you. Say, "The more I trust, the more I shine!"

What would it feel like if you remembered your wholeness, your magic, your greatness, your powerful, beautiful essence? How would it feel to know how divine love feels? How would it feel to know that you don't need anything outside yourself to validate you? Remember that right where you are in every moment is where you were meant to be. That means you can take a deep breath and relax. Millions of people need you to be you and to let your light shine.

I was watching an episode of *Super Soul Sunday* on the OWN network, and Oprah was interviewing an author. I was listening to him, impressed by his intelligence and wisdom. My mind had the thought, *he's so poetic and deeply philosophical. I'm not like that.* And then the next day in my meditation, this thought came to me: *My readers and audiences need me to be exactly who I am, because the energy of who I am resonates with them.* And that's why you need to be happy being you: the people in your world *need* you to be you. You have a specific essence, which is divinely orchestrated, which resonates with the people who are attracted to you.

Love is infinite. *You* are infinite. To connect with yourself and feel your divine nature of empowerment, fully embrace and accept who you are as a divine being. Say, "I am an infinite, divine being. I choose to awaken to the truth of who I am. I step into my radiance and expand my energy. I'm committed to being my beautiful and powerful light. I step into my sovereign being, and I choose to believe in myself with all my heart and soul!"

A previous workshop attendee asked me, "Do you believe that we are whole?" And, I replied, "Yes, we are whole individuals and interconnected with the wholeness of everything." You are always connected to the Divine, and the Divine's essence is part of you. We forgot who we were. Now we are remembering. That is why it's so vitally important to manage our emotional state and take responsibility and process our repressed hurts, disappointments, anger, jealousies, and traumas. That is the way to love, acceptance, and peace. You are love. You don't need to prove it or beg for it—it's who you already are right now. When we can process these lower-vibrating emotions we then create beliefs that support our divine being, and live more lightly because we aren't feeling drained or wasting our energy.

Over the years, many people have said to me, "I was taught not to say nice things to myself, because that's considered being conceited and self-absorbed." But being unconditionally loving to yourself is *not* a feeling of being better than or above others. That's operating from egotism. Think of unconditional love has an energy vibration. Unconditional love is a very high, or fast, energy vibration. And the love that we have allowed ourselves to feel is exactly how much love we are genuinely able to express to the world. Someone who is emotionally wounded and reacting through suffering is occupied predominantly with a "how can I get" vibe. A person who is balanced in healthy self-love, on the other hand, has the ability to *give* that same amount of healthy love.

Unconditional love is pure, beautiful, kind, caring, and loving. It's not defensive, divisive, controlling, manipulative, or critical. For most of my younger life, when it came to my religion, I felt judged and "less than," which caused feelings of separation. We all have felt that way at one time or another, and it's not a good way to feel. We are done with the abusive nature, the tearing down of people, and the bullying. We are moving into a more loving way of building people up, encouraging, connecting, helping people shine and feel included and needed—equality among all humans, and a state of reverence for all. Doesn't that feel so much better? Breathe that energy into you.

Living as an infinite being, *KNOWING* unconditional love is our natural essence, we adopt new philosophies that ask not how we can *punish* people, but how can we see people as beautiful, interesting, divine, whole beings. How can we understand that another person's reality is the best thing for their evolutionary process? How can we see ourselves as divine, infinitely powerful beings? How can we help heal people instead of lock them up and throw away the key? How can we focus on health and vibrancy?

Norway's Halden Prison is called the most humane prison in the world. The corrections officers treat the prisoners with respect and dignity. Their focus is on rehabilitation and healing. It's not about revenge; it's about bringing back into society someone who would make a good neighbor and a productive citizen. The prisoners are encouraged to work, learn, and be active. The prison staff are trained and schooled to mentor and coach the inmates. There isn't much violence in this prison.

When people demonstrate harmful behavior to others, this is indication that they have lost their way. They are suffering and disconnected from their inner source and sovereignty, and they are in enormous emotional pain. Such a person's body, spirit, and mind need healing. This Norwegian correctional institution understands that prisoners need healing as part of their rehabilitation, especially since the vast majority of them are introduced back into society. People hurt others because they themselves are suffering. For this reason, it's imperative that we introduce correctional programs that help heal people.

To create peace on earth, each of us must make peace within our own heart first. Because everything is energy, in each moment our state of being dictates our vibration. Our thoughts are electrical, and they stimulate our emotions, which create an energetic field. This energetic field is attracting to us similar frequencies to those it emits. Fear is the lowest, or densest vibration. With this understanding, we are managing our focus, our intention, and our thoughts because we understand that our emotions play a role in creating our reality. What helps me not identify and attach to my emotions is thinking of them as vibrations. So I say to myself, "right now this vibration that is flowing through me is sadness. I accept you. It doesn't feel good right now, but I know you are showing me something." For me, thinking of emotions as higher vibrating and lower vibrating is more helpful than labeling as good and bad. Don't beat yourself up if you are unhappy. Express love to yourself by allowing your emotions to be without resistance and trust this soon will pass. Ask, "Why do I feel this way?" Listen to what you hear and sense. Now say, "I am aware of my divine, infinite powers as a human and spiritual being. I align my intentions with my higher self and connect with the love from the Divine. I choose to create new, healthier beliefs and expand my limited views. I choose to be the light that I am, and *feel* the light that I am: my divine nature. My intention is to unhook from the story, from the drama and all the limited thinking. I'm choosing to remember that I'm an infinite being and I'm ALWAYS connected to my core, to unconditional love within me and above."

I have spent many years learning about empowerment and unconditional love. This is not something we were taught. We were taught to disconnect from our feelings and emotions, to "suck it up," be strong, and keep a stiff upper lip—and to compare. In the business world, we are taught to be aggressive, to use force, to win above all else, without any regard for others. We are taught to compete, not to cocreate and collaborate. We are taught a "lack" mentality—that there's not enough to go around. We were taught fear. And now we are learning to value ourselves and all that we offer to the world in a place of trust—to drop our walls of self-protection, drop our burden of self-doubt, and awaken to our heart's essence.

The generations before us were groping their way through their own cobwebs of insecurity, feelings of separation, pain, and fear, doing the best they knew how. As we all expand inward, moving into loving and appreciating our beautiful being, we are experiencing life lighter, freer, and with greater joy.

How do we move back to a state of unconditional love and inner peace for ourselves? First, we remember the powerful beings that we are, and who created us: the Divine. Love has no bottom. It cannot run out, and no one can take it from you. You are eternal light and consciousness. That means you are a magnificent, divine being that is everlasting—and that is good news indeed for the planet! Set your intention: "I intend to see myself through the eyes of unconditional love. I affirm the truth of myself, who was made in the image of the Divine. I claim the divinity that is within me! I believe in an infinite reality, that there is enough for all."

In exploring who we are and why we are here, we ask questions such as "Where does true fulfillment come from?" After many years of self-discovery and observation, I've found that it doesn't come just from making a nice income or getting lofty job titles, degrees, or certifications. Explore what it means to you. Maybe for you, fulfillment comes from living an authentic life, being yourself and liking yourself, doing what you love, building happy relationships, helping people, making a difference, feeling needed and connected to something greater than yourself, being happy with who you are, and being financially able to support a comfortable lifestyle.

Living with love as your focus, begin to explore your beliefs by asking yourself the right questions. Take out your journal and write your responses to these questions: "What belief system does not serve my highest good? What beliefs are aligned with unconditionally loving myself? How can I open my mind and heart to live in the highest way possible? What does my heart need from me? If I believed that my path truly existed and was just for me, and if I truly believed in myself, how would I believe and think? From a place of feeling my own wholeness, how can I see this situation in the highest and best light? How would the Divine see this situation? How would my wiser self see this situation? How can I open my heart and allow myself to feel more love? How can I live in the most authentic way?"

To prepare yourself for opening your heart, begin by stating an intention: "I am ready to open up and expand deeper into my heart. I choose to see myself through the eyes of unconditional love. I choose to be an expression of love by acting grateful, compassionate and kind. I choose to expand my love to more people, to animals, to nature, and to myself. I choose to feel the beautiful new energies of the divine love that is here on earth." With this intention, you are open to increasing the intensity of your love and the number of people you share your love with. You are prepared to observe what stands in the way of your being a pure, vulnerable heart.

You give yourself this choice by agreeing that you are responsible for your thoughts, beliefs, actions, emotions, and perceptions. And through your own choosing and observation, you can tune in to your emotions and sense whether the way you are feeling feels good for you. Many books and speakers talk about how important it is to take responsibility. Have you stopped to think exactly what that means? What that means energetically? We are constantly making choices and agreements in what we believe, what we accept, and what we don't accept. Even by *not* responding to something, we are making a choice. We also allow others to make choices for us. The energy of what we embody is what we draw to us.

Until we create heaven on earth, we will have many experiences to practice managing our minds. Over time, you will become a master of your thoughts, feelings, emotions, beliefs, perceptions, and experiences. We are untangling ourselves from all the fear-based systems.

To live with a heart-and-mind presence of unconditional love means we have an intention of accepting situations, people, and ourselves just as we are. We are open to what others have to say. We can view everything in an open space of curiosity and interest. We don't have to express an opposing opinion. In this state, we are freer to move fluidly and fully experience the energies of life. In this openness, we cultivate being the witness more and more throughout our life. We have less emotional charge and more inner peace. This state of being is for others and for us. And we know that we have choice in our thoughts. We ask, *what thought would create a better feeling? What thought is aligned with my desires? What thought keeps me in a place of unconditional love?*

Humans can live on earth and be happy, peaceful, and healthy. Without realizing it, we have *settled* for way too long. We have settled within our definition of who we are. We have settled to please our parents. We have settled out of fear. We have even settled and conformed to fit in, to be liked, and to live in a way that is not aligned with our heart. We have spent way too much time focused on the things we don't like. We have settled for a limited perception of ourselves. And now we are coming into our beautiful power of what it means to be a magnificent, luminous human being. We understand that it is not just on rare occasions that we are meant to experience happy and peaceful moments. It is meant to be the normal reality of our existence. Can you imagine your life this way: being peaceful and happy during most of your waking life? Are you open and ready to live this way? If so, say, "I am open to being happy and peaceful as my normal way of living." As you say that, see what comes up for you. Are you a little afraid that it won't last? Does it make you sad because your heart longs to be happy and live a peaceful life? Do you feel deserving of this happiness? Yes, you are 100 percent deserving!

Living Powerfully

You are the official authority of yourself. From a place of empowerment, you learn in a more conscious way without the need to suffer. Suffering comes from a victim mentality of resistance and holding on to pain for long periods of time. Living fully empowered, we become much more responsible in processing our fear, sadness, and worries, and we take accountability for our minds, emotions, bodies, and actions. The processing of our emotions is crucial. We are learning to manage our emotions, to feel them and transmute them into compassion and love. Learning how to process our emotions builds our empowerment and confidence.

We are stepping into our full sovereignty and owning our infinite grandeur. It's time to own the divine connection to spirit that runs through us and around us. Independent of the masses, we can choose not to follow what others are saying, turn off our television news programs, and disengage from the fear the media are selling to us. We learn to draw our energy back to ourselves and depend on our inner world for validation, direction, and guidance. We are "inner led" and have the courage to live in a way that is harmonious to us, and we place value on what is important to us. Say, "I am learning to depend on myself for validation, direction, and guidance. I choose to broaden my identity and connect with my soul's purpose."

The more I placed my intention on my spiritual growth, the more life gave me opportunities to tune in and see where and how I was giving my power away, and how to connect back to myself. The more we allow ourselves to feel a connection within, the more it feels like home. Our emotional attachments can consist of unhealthy habits; unhealthy jobs or careers; limiting relationships, fears, perspectives, and insecurities. These attachments come from our denying our beautiful, authentic identity. As we are going through uncomfortable situations, it's important to remember, this process is what enables us to see if there is a better path, a better way to feel, to believe, to perceive. Indeed, this is the path to freedom of the mind! And as these attachments lose their grip on us and dissolve, we find ourselves in a space of more openness, expanding into more parts of ourselves and the universe. We are on the path to inner peace.

We are spiritual beings in a human body, having a spiritual experience. And as spirit beings, we are always connected to the Divine. You hold a unique piece of heaven inside you. It's time to stop being a passenger through life, get behind the wheel, and drive with both hands. This means waking up to the understanding that you can choose a reality based on living powerfully. And living powerfully means we are responsible for our minds: thinking, choosing, and creating the reality we place ourselves in. By changing our awareness, we change our reality. By untangling the unhealthy beliefs and processing our fears and emotional attachments and programs, we set ourselves free. A fully empowered person understands that we don't need permission from something outside ourselves to move forward in the direction of our joy and heart's desires. We don't need something outside us to fill ourselves up. We can generate joy and love from within. We know that we chose this earthly life. And we navigate our energy by moving toward what we agree with, and leaving behind what we don't agree with.

Each time we feel uncomfortable and take action that expresses our nonagreement with a particular behavior, it's as if we are saying, "This is not acceptable. I don't agree with this behavior. I will not tolerate this." And we move our energy toward what we *do* agree with. The actions of standing up for what you agree with—and standing against what you don't agree with—build your inner strength and self-reliance. Your body expresses to you how it feels. Trust what you intuit and sense in your own body. Your body is a tool that navigates you either *toward* or *away from* something or someone. The emotions that you feel in your body are a useful tool showing you what wants to be healed within you.

> *"The love you feel in life is a reflection of the love you feel in yourself."*
>
> —Deepak Chopra

Living as a fully empowered being, you are being diligently responsible for your actions and thoughts. In the moment that your mind is aware of a little fear, you KNOW that you are now standing in front of a split between two paved roads. Executing your free will, you make a conscious choice. To the right is the road from your past. This is a road of great familiarity—it's the road of anxiousness, worry, and fear. It will be very easy to head down this road again, and whenever you do, your body will be familiar with the chemicals secreted by the fear and worry. But you have another choice. To the left is a *new* road, being graded and paved right now. This is the road of peace, trust, love, and the path of harmony. As you learn to be the master of your mind by choosing thoughts that create peace and calm within, you practice taking the road on your left. And the more you take this road, the smoother and better paved it becomes, until it becomes the natural route and response for your body to take and to make. This builds a momentum of empowerment. And eventually, it becomes the road *most* traveled. The road on the left says, "I trust my life path. I am doing great. I'm strong. I am exactly where I'm meant to be. I'm proud of myself. I'm powerful. I'm great. I unconditionally love myself, and I believe in *me*." I noticed that I was putting too much emphasis on fear, and I realized that I was making myself a victim of my fear. So I said, "I am not a victim to my fear. I'm much bigger and more powerful, and I choose to live in LOVE!"

Choosing a reality of knowing that you are unconditional love and light means recognizing that you are not at the mercy of anyone or anything, and that you are not at the mercy of your own fears. As an adult, you don't need to be validated anymore by a parent or a partner. You have the courage to observe and listen to your fears, insecurities, and disappointments. Each time you recognize that you have an emotional charge, ask the emotion, "What do you want to say to me?" And tell it, "I accept you." Allow it a voice, and then bathe it in love. You must understand this intellectually and feel this inside your body, as a belief system inside your cells. The Divine created a perfect system of divine energetic laws, and humans have the capacity to live in harmony within this divine system. Choose to believe that you are this powerful, and you can live in a loving reality where life flows easily and smoothly. This is the next step in our human evolution, and you chose to be here now, to be on this ride of expansion of your divine light in a human body!

"Always aim at complete harmony of thought and word and deed. Always aim at purifying your thoughts, and everything will be well."

—Mahatma Gandhi

Conditional Love: Fears

During a workshop, an attendee said she didn't have any fears. And then she later admitted to me that she was not aware that even little worries and concerns are fears. In our past, for many of us, myself included, our dominant "muscle" was to worry. I was in a discussion with a young man who was sharing with me his career ideas, and then all his worries came pouring out. I said, "Trust. If you're being led to pursue your ideas, everything will fall into place at the right time." I asked him whether this was something he was passionate about, and I asked him what was driving him to go in this direction.

To build trust within ourselves, it's imperative that we allow ourselves time to sit quietly, go within, and connect with our inner voice—with our higher self and with our heart. And from that space, we can follow our intuition and trust. Here is a lesson in trusting intuition and life: I was giving a private yoga lesson to a woman. During the class I received strong insight that this yoga student was very intuitive but she didn't know it. I had the feeling that I was being guided to tell her. I thought to myself, "How do I just come out with this message?" I allowed life to present itself to me. And, there it was-- perfect timing! Later on in the class, I had the thought, "I wonder if she is on any pharmaceuticals?" And, then she said, "I'm only on one pharmaceutical". It was as if she read my mind! So I told her she is so intuitive because she picked up on my thought. I told her I just had the thought about her and pharmaceuticals. I asked her if she realized how intuitive she is. Her face lit up!! I asked her if she is very sensitive and has been her whole life. And, she replied, yes. For some reason, I felt it was important for her to realize and appreciate her intuitive abilities. It was so amazing to see her face light up! These are moments that touch my heart and stay with me. I pass this message on to you. Pay attention to your intuitive abilities. You may be much more intuitive and guided than you believe. Do you appreciate your intuitive sense?

If a fear or worry pops in, catch yourself and ask, *what could go right? How would you feel if everything did go right?* We are trained to focus automatically on what could go wrong. The world of full empowerment focuses on imagining the best-case scenario and then letting it go and trusting.

Fear is the opposite of empowerment. Each time we blame someone or something or feel we have been wronged in some way, we give our power away and become a victim. And we often do this without even being aware of it. We are making that person or situation outside ourselves more powerful than *we* are. It is a belief system that says something outside ourselves is to blame for how we feel. It's a position of not owning our innate power.

An attachment can also stem from a fear-based belief that we think we need something, such as security, love, or happiness, from another person outside ourselves. In falling for this belief, we are being conditional to ourselves. We are buying into, and believing in, a system that is controlling us. We have just given our power away to fear—to an insecurity, an attachment, an expectation, a personalization. We have veered away from our connection to our beautiful and infinite core essence. Fear comes to us in many guises. It may be fear of the unknown. *How am I going to make things happen? Am I going to meet a new lover or a new best friend? Will I find a new job that I like? Will I get new clients?* We may fear a future event that may or may not occur, fear not being good enough or not being liked or accepted. We may fear failure, fear losing love, fear hurting someone's feelings, or fear that someone is going to be mad at us. Or we may even fear our own power.

Many of society's systems are set up in a way that perpetuates a fear-based reality. We buy insurance in the event we should get sick someday, insurance just in case we get into an accident, insurance on our life, professional liability insurance, insurance for our homes and rental properties, pet insurance, airline insurance, moving insurance, dental insurance, automobile towing insurance. In fact, we pay hundreds or even thousands of dollars a month just in case something bad should happen to us. Now, *that's* putting money and energy into a fear-based system. The question is, if you put that much into fearing the worst, how much do you invest in loving yourself? After all, to choose a reality of love versus fear is to move back to our natural, divine state of being—the way we were intended to be. I'm not saying to stop funding the insurance industry. I *am* saying to begin to see where your energy is flowing and how much of your energy is invested in the false reality of a fear-based existence, and how much is invested in your true nature of unconditional love. Begin to observe the energy of people around you, and people you listen to in the media. Are they entrenched in a fear-based model, or in a model anchored in love, empowerment, and trust?

To begin to move out of this energy, we observe where our energy and money is going. Money is energy. We know how powerful we are, and we can choose to spend more of our energy on things that are life sustaining. We can invest in eating healthy foods, planting our own vegetable and flower gardens, exercising, living "green," helping and encouraging others, volunteering, learning, joining organizations and groups that support a loving world, practicing yoga and meditation, and spending time in nature or any other enjoyable hobby or interest.

In a state of conditional love, we are not living fully in the moment, not owning our divinity. Rather, we are operating from a sense of lack: feeling that we are limited, not good enough, not deserving or worthy. We fear that we "did something wrong" and that love can be taken away from us. This is because most of us were not taught from birth who we really are and how powerful we are. And we are now learning the way back to ourselves. Remember, everything is in divine order. The universe is organized for you to be happy.

*"Your task is not to seek for love,
but merely to seek and find all the barriers within yourself
that you have built against it."*

—Rumi

Take-Away Exercises: Unconditional Love

Centering Yourself in Unconditional Love

Sit and relax. Close your eyes, and spend a couple of minutes taking deep belly breaths, in through your nose and out through your mouth. Visualize connecting to the energy of the Divine: pure love and light. Connect with your image that represents unconditional love. Set your intention: "I ask and intend to be connected to the divine love and light and to my higher self, to become one with this love and light and feel it inside my heart." Feel this love inside every part of your being. Say, "I choose to expand my ability to feel divine love. I feel this love in my cells. My cells are lighting up in response. I feel this love in my heart, in my blood and bones. I am love. God loves me. I feel love. I love God. I embrace my identity as pure love and light. I am a unique soul signature of the Divine."

Appreciation Visualization

There are hundreds of things to appreciate at any moment. Verbalize your gratitude within yourself and with others all day long. Include things that you like and find valuable about yourself.

2

OBSERVING ATTACHMENTS AND PROCESSING EMOTIONS

It's vitally important to observe all the ways we give our power away and feel separate from our own light. We perceive the world based on our own relationship with self. We grew up in a world that taught us to value ourselves externally by our achievements, material things, the money we make, the prestige attached to our jobs, and what other people think and believe about us. And *all* those things are transitory. We were taught to stay in a box and live according to society's conventions. We are learning to seek love from within, which is a new concept for many of us.

I was walking with a neighbor, telling her about this book, *Language of the Heart,* and she asked me what it is about. I replied, "unconditional love," and she said, "Oh, it's so hard to find it out there." I looked at her with a smile on my face and replied, "That's because, like most of us, you're looking in the wrong place, it's *within*." Oh-h-h-h," she said, and laughed. Teasing her, I put my hand on my forehead and said, "You're like the book *Where's Waldo?* Only the question is, *where is unconditional love?*"

If we expect others to fulfill and validate us, life situations are going to come up, and people are going to say and do things, that reflect back to us how we feel. If we are praying for a special someone to come into our life because we think this will bring us happiness, then we will draw to us an experience with happiness vibrating at that level. If, on the other hand, our desire is to be happy and content within, to feel whole, we draw to us an equal. It's imperative to build and connect our sense of self from within. This is the foundation that we ground ourselves in.

Our fulfillment comes from more than one source because we have a variety of interests. No one person is meant to fill up our heart and be the answer to all our needs. This is why we have many different interests, hobbies, passions, and connections with other people, with pets, and with nature, but true, everlasting fulfillment comes from within.

> *"If you look to others for fulfillment, you will never truly be fulfilled. If your happiness depends on money, you will never be happy with yourself. Be content with what you have; rejoice in the way things are. When you realize there is nothing lacking, the whole world belongs to you."*
>
> —Lao Tzu

You may notice a particular theme that repeats itself from one of your relationships to another. The gift to ourselves happens when we acknowledge the theme, because in that moment, we let ourselves in on what needs to be healed within us. The healing always brings us back to our wholeness. All your life situations have helped you grow. Every disappointment I had was a result of my own attachment, fear, and expectation. You may be wondering, *so what is an attachment?* In this book, we can define attachments as emotions that are invested in something—a personal buy-in to a specific outcome—or expectations we place on others or on something outside ourselves to fulfill our own desires or needs. We apply a high level of importance and *meaning* to specific beliefs that create our emotional attachments.

If we are relying on someone or something outside ourselves to bring us joy, security, or happiness or to tell us that we matter, and we don't receive the outcome we were looking for, then our well-being is compromised. By attaching with something outside ourselves, we have given our power away. Have you ever had this experience? Someone tells you, "I love you," and then they wait for you to say it back. And if you don't, they repeat it, maybe a little louder or more insistently: "I love you." They know you heard them, but they have an expectation and a *need* for you to fill them up by saying it back. The less attached we are, the freer and more empowered we are to live as our authentic and powerful selves. We learn to fill ourselves up. And actually, we are *already* filled; we just don't remember.

A workshop attendee asked me if there was a difference between a *need* and a *want*. Let's not confuse a need in this sense with our basic human needs. I'm referring to "need" in the context of wanting something outside ourselves to make us feel good because we have a sense of lack, insecurity, or not being enough as we are in that moment. Yes, there is a difference. If we have an expectation from a needy place within us, and the expectation isn't met, we may feel resentful and perhaps even angry. We are looking for some kind of validation from outside, and if we don't get it, we feel cheated. A want is a desire—something that we as humans will always have. It is our desires that help us move forward.

Here's a perfect example: A woman named Sara made the decision to help someone out, and took the day off from work to do so. She felt put-upon and really needed and expected to feel appreciated. Sara was thinking to herself, *he really had better appreciate me because I took the day off from work to take care of him.* Well, suppose he doesn't express to Sara enough appreciation to satisfy Sara's need. Sara is going to be resentful and angry. Her emotions of resentment and anger will energetically draw opportunities to experience *more* resentment and anger. She is bound by her resentment. Sara has a belief that she needs something outside herself to feel appreciated.

Let's compare this scenario to one without a need and expectation. Sara wants to help a family member out, and her focus and intention is on sharing from a place of love, genuine caring, and joy. Sara willingly gives with a pure heart. In this scenario, she isn't focused on getting something to fill her up. She doesn't *need* anything. Thus, she doesn't feel put-upon. Her intention is on the joy and love of helping. And she feels good about herself. If we really trust life, we understand that giving love with no expectations brings love back to us. This is part of energetic spiritual law. The universe is divinely orchestrated with specific energetic laws. When our intention and emotions for helping are not attached to any specific outcome we receive the same purity back in one way or another.

Our vibration aligns with a matched experience. I know this can be very challenging when caring for people who take others for granted and don't show appreciation. In this case, we can use this as an experiment to observe our own energy and intention. We are responsible only for our own energy. It's imperative to align our choices with a pure heart. And if we really don't want to do something, we have the choice not to do it, or we can change our perspective.

As we grow in our self-love we see with clear, fresh eyes. We remember that we are beautiful, divine beings that are made up of pure love, and when we recognize this we will not vibrate with a neediness that settles for tiny, infrequent, scattered morsels of love. We allow divine universal love and light to flow *through* us, and we connect with and expand our own inner light and begin to live more in our hearts. Set your intention: "I am open to explore my attachments." Exploring your attachments gives you a clear picture of where your energy and personal power are going. And then you uncover the beliefs you have that are creating the attachment. Choosing to expand or change to higher vibrational beliefs is recognizing our freedom of choice. The more you are connected through awareness to your true, authentic self, the more clearly you can see your conditional behavior and how you compromise yourself. Detachment allows us to make the highest choices, with adaptability and flexibility, keeping our energy grounded and centered within, with less emotional charge. With detachment, we find our way by trusting our divine inner light, and we choose to be grounded within this light. We trust the universe's divine orchestration and our own powerful abilities. In a place of detachment, we are not personalizing life scenarios—we are free! Here's a good prayer to use: "I choose to live in the highest and best way possible."

A fear is showing us that it's time to change to a new belief—one aligned with our beautiful sovereignty. When you are fearful say, "I invite space in between my drama—my fear—and me. I invite love, joy, and trust into the situation. I remind myself of my wholeness, my infinite power, the truth of who I am: unconditional love and divine, infinite potential. I accept this situation fully. This is an experience that I am having now. I choose a state of neutrality and peace. I increase my power and inner strength and expand it." Now sit outside in nature and take several deep belly breaths. Ask yourself, "What is the highest way to believe that recognizes my own sovereignty?"

"The root cause of all attachment is lack of love."

—Sri Amma Bhagavan

Observing Attachments and Processing Emotions

When you believe that everything is in divine order, your attachment recedes and you trust that this situation is expanding your awareness. You trust that you are learning something. You trust your life. You trust yourself and your connection to the whole universe. You trust your own manifesting abilities and all the good things that await you. You begin to take things, situations, and yourself a lot more lightly. You have less emotional charge toward things. You bring yourself back to unconditional love. You open and allow love and trust into the situation.

We have expectations of how things should be, how we should be perceived, and how others should act. And we have these expectations for ourselves. The problem is, when we hold on so tightly to our expectations we are setting ourselves up for disappointment. The more fluid we can be with life, and the more we go with the flow, the more we detach, fully accepting and embracing what is. The more likely we are to stay peaceful. Pause for a moment and just imagine that the world is set up for you to succeed in it. And that what you are seeking is seeking you!

To live life with a focus on unconditional love, we begin by untangling our own personal emotional attachments. Each time you release from an attachment you become more awakened to your ability to truly love yourself and believe that you are worthy of happiness. You deserve to live in a way that honors your soul's calling and purpose. You are worthy of being yourself in all your relationships! You are an equal. You deserve to enjoy life! Remember, we are done with the mentality of suffering and judgment. Stop judging yourself. Allow yourself to be.

If we are not diligent, our mind may be wrapped up in things that compromise our space of unconditional love, such as wondering whether someone likes us or identifying ourselves with a job title, or our accomplishments or why someone is rude to us, or looking for love outside ourselves. And maybe we have spent way too many years yearning for Dad's approval, getting upset if we don't get our way, or being scared of the unknown. Other attachments might include being ashamed to admit your real age. A more unconditionally loving attitude would be one of "I couldn't care less; I'm proud to be forty-seven years old" (or thirty-seven, or seventy-seven). This is an attitude of empowerment, since you are not giving your energy away to the fear of how someone else is going to respond. You deserve to be with people who don't have a judgment about your age. Another common attachment is being concerned with holding on to beauty and looking young. This can be very energy draining.

"You lose only what you cling to."

—the Buddha

Putting light on our attachments brings things to our awareness, and then we have a choice to open up to a new perspective and belief. We are healing the division within ourselves—the part of us that forgot our wholeness, our personal power, and our beautiful, divine potential. As you read through this section on emotional attachments, notice whether you identify with some of these stories. It's important that you connect with your own authentic feelings and emotions. At the end of this chapter, do the "Exercise for Processing Emotions" for each concern, fear, or uncomfortable feeling. I recommend using the meridian-tapping technique, too. (I don't teach the technique in this book, but it's very easy to get the information on the Internet.)

After each attachment scenario, I offer a perspective of unconditional-love beliefs, affirmations, and intentions for you to try as a new, expanded way to see your life. Uncovering the beliefs and feelings behind your attachments is key. It's crucially important. Beliefs are assumed truths. They are precepts by which we live our life. If we think these thoughts over and over again, our body reacts with an automatic response. The qualities of our thoughts shape the wiring in our brain. The mind, spirit, and body are interconnected. We can be attached to our beliefs. And our beliefs have emotional control over us.

We adopted many of our beliefs in childhood, from a parent and our environment. Thus, they are not really ours. As we evolve, we begin to lighten up on our beliefs, specifically the ones that don't serve our highest good. We can change our beliefs and remove the programs that don't serve us, and choose to let them float away while we stay in the present moment. To move into a higher belief system, ask, "What is the most empowering interpretation?" This is a space of feeling love for others and yourself.

Affirmations are positive, sustaining thoughts. Affirming statements bring you into your power. You must believe what you are saying. Choose and repeat the affirming statements that have a resonance for you. There are many affirming statements, and each one has a different frequency. A person who has low self-esteem may begin with the affirming statement "I am learning how to become a friend to myself." Someone who has good self-esteem may use a similar affirming statement: I completely love and appreciate who I am right now, in all ways. There is no judgment, whether you are just beginning to learn how to love yourself, or already do! I'm proud of you for having the insight that this is really important work for your well-being. Thank you for having the courage to be honest with yourself and for wanting to grow in self-love. When we truly know who we are as beautiful, powerful divine beings, we won't need to practice affirmations. But in the meantime, since we are moving into a new way of feeling about life and about ourselves, we must practice.

Intentions are energies focused toward a desired way to be, feel, create, and act. Writing and vocalizing our intentions sets energy in motion, drawing to us that which we desire and placing us in that intended vibration. We must feel this inside ourselves by expressing this emotion, this vibration. By the law of attraction, we draw that vibration back to us as long as it is the dominant vibration that we carry within us. That's why it's so important to be aware of what you are thinking, feeling, and believing.

To get the most out of this section, be present with your own feelings. Set your intention to be open to the suggestive

beliefs, affirmations, and intentions of unconditional love. Choose the one's that resonate the most with you or create your own. It's important that you not only believe the suggestive beliefs, affirmations and intentions but you feel them in your body as a *knowing*. As you are reading them, if you have feelings of doubts or any resistance or fears, use the Processing Emotions Exercise at the end of the chapter.

Common Scenarios of Emotional Attachments

Attachment to Identifying with a Job

I remember when I got fired from a job at age twenty-nine. I was devastated. I felt rejected by the world and was terribly sad and fearful. At that point in my life, I valued myself according to the amount of money I was making—a learned belief system that I had adopted from my environment. For a couple of months, I had no income. I felt terrible. I was critical and judgmental of myself. This was a very challenging couple of months, right up until I found a job. I felt that the world didn't need or love me. I was taking this situation very personally. I felt like a failure. My self-worth was connected to my financial success. During these two months, I was diligently searching for a job. I landed a two-month "in the meantime" job until I received an offer that ended up setting me on a wonderful new career path. I stayed there for eight years. This job gave me many wonderful opportunities, including a move across the country, world travel, and growth into a vice presidency in the company.

Getting fired may feel like an awful event when it occurs, because we are caught up in feelings of rejection, fear of the unknown, and the trap of valuing ourselves by external measures. This is a perfect example of attachment.

If we can make a conscious decision not to personalize, not to allow this to devalue us, we can trust divine orchestration and trust that there is another door opening and that our time in the old situation is done. This will allow us to flow peacefully through life.

During the two months of looking for a job, I was also on a spiritual quest, which created an expansion into my heart. This quest propelled me into seeking and reading spiritual books, attending healing workshops, and expanding my mind. We can go through the ending of one cycle and begin another with peace. We don't have to create suffering.

We are far more than our job titles. It is much more important to be connected within, to let our joyful desires determine our path, and to flow with the current of life.

Trust that your energy attracts all your heart's desires. When a situation doesn't work out the way you expected, trust that it was meant to be for that finite time. And when you are ready for new experiences you will attract new situations and people to move you along your life path. From a place of unconditional love, you can live more in a state of accepting what is occurring in that moment. Trust that you are exactly where you are meant to be in every moment.

Unconditional-Love Beliefs: I trust that there is a higher purpose for this situation and I see the perfection. I'm being redirected to a new experience. A new beginning is unfolding. This transition period is an opportunity for me to regroup, be still, stay in the moment, and allow and accept this process. I am meant to be sharing my energy and talents somewhere else. My energy is done here. I'm grateful for the experience. I trust that I will take all my lessons with me, and I know that a new door is opening for me that is for my highest and best good, mutually beneficial for everyone, and at the best timing for all parties involved. Even though I felt rejected, I choose not to reject myself. I have everything I need to fulfill my life's purpose. I'm very excited for the amazing connections on the near horizon, and amazing career opportunities that lie ahead. I'm creating my next experience now. My new opportunity is pulling me toward it. I trust my intuition and know that I'm guided toward my best and highest good. I accept this moment fully.

Affirmations: I am relaxed. I am calm. I am valuable to the whole universe. I'm much more than my job title. I trust my life's path! I deeply and completely love myself. I'm looking forward to my next adventure. I am a wiz at manifesting, and I trust that I will manifest my next career opportunity. I'm focused on living in a way that is aligned with my heart.

> *Intentions:* I ask and intend to be connected to my light and inner power. I intend to learn from this situation and to live fully in the moment, with trust and faith. I intend to face the day with wonder, love and an open heart. I intend to see all possibilities and probabilities for life right now. I intend to make connections. I attract to me the career and the job that is mutually beneficial to all. I intend to stay aligned with all the frequencies that support my highest good and stay open. I choose to flow through my life peacefully and live in the present moment. I ask and intend for reassurance and particular signs to help lead me in the best and highest direction.

Attachment to Money

I had a client who was extremely attached to making money. It was her overriding focus, and she lived for years feeling as if she never had enough. She identified her self-worth with money, so that when she was making good money she was on a high, and when she wasn't she was unhappy with herself. She lived in fear, emotionally attached to each prospect and each client who entered or left her business. She was angry each time a prospect didn't become a client, and each time a client moved on. She was giving conditional love to herself.

Money is energy, nothing more and nothing less. We are energetic beings. The relationship you have with money is based on what you believe about money. Do you envy wealthy people? Are you comfortable around wealthy people? Do you believe you are worthy of lots of money? Do you believe there is enough to go around? Explore the relationship you have with money. Do you trust that money can flow easily and effortlessly to you? Do you appreciate what you do have? Do you have trust in yourself? Do you believe that you live in an abundant universe and that you are abundant? Are you at the mercy of life, or are you a cocreator? Do you think you are above others because you have a lot of money?

If we are grateful for all of what life offers through the exchange of money, then money flows more easily to us. If our belief system is focused on the lack of it, this will show in the way money flows in our life. Practice really feeling grateful for and worthy of the things your money buys—the food and shelter, each dollar that you receive, and each bill you pay. Say, "Thank you, universe, for all the money that pours forth in my life and for all the wonderful things I can buy with it, create with it, and share with others. Thank you for all the comfort, safety, well-being, and joy that it brings into my life and other lives. I am GRATEFUL."

The value of who we are is not measured by the amount of money we make. True fulfillment comes from aligning our heart with our actions and having the courage to create and live an empowered, authentic life. And to trust fully in our own sovereignty means we KNOW that the universe supports us. We need to support ourselves by believing and trusting. Fulfillment also comes from feeling that we are responsible, loving, good people, leaving a footprint of love, joy, integrity, generosity, and happiness behind us. We are here to experience joy, express ourselves, learn and grow, connect with others, and allow our inner light to shine and enhance our soul. We don't need anything to prove our worthiness, especially if it means allowing others to take away anything from who we are.

Instead of pinning our success on the amount of money we make, we would do better to focus on how abundant and joyful our heart feels. An abundant heart is richer than any amount of money. Abundance is the sum of *all* the ways the universe gives to us. The universe gives to us daily. Pay attention to every thank-you you receive, for this is the energy of appreciation coming to you. Pay attention to each act of kindness bestowed on you: someone gave you a book of healthy recipes; someone bought you a shirt; in an emergency your neighbor drove you to urgent care; a friend walked your dog or bought you groceries. Do you block the help the universe is offering, by dismissing help or ignoring it? Do you allow this energy into your heart? This is abundance entering your life. However much love, kindness, support, encouragement, and compassion we put out is the same amount that flows back to us. Pay attention to the kind words, the inspiring information—any gift given, however small or ordinary. Did you see a lucky penny on the street? Did someone offer to barter with you, sharing in the exchange of services? Is a business associate helping you out with talents, services, advice, and skills?

Abundance has its own energy. An abundant heart feels plentiful, amply supplied by the universe. As divine beings, we trust that we are living in an abundant universe.

A client of mine was in tight financial straits, and I suggested a barter exchange between her and another businessperson. But my client's mind was so focused on "making money," she couldn't see the opportunity. Money is just one avenue of receiving. And no amount of money can buy an abundant heart! The way I look at it, why limit ourselves? Our unseen divine, loving helpers are very creative.

Unconditional-Love Beliefs: I love money. My heart feels rich. I trust that the perfect clients arrive in my life at the perfect time. I really value what I offer. My essence brings value to the world. My self-worth is independent of the amount of money I have in the bank. I value myself no matter how much money I have in the bank. I know that I have financial power. Money is wonderful! It allows me to eat healthy foods to keep my body healthy, to feel safe, to help others, buy healthy products, be creative and express my joy and passions, give wonderful gifts to people, and travel to amazing places.

Affirmations: I am secure and safe. I am deserving and worthy of money. I'm an energetic match to lots of money flowing to me. I graciously receive it. I'm abundant and rich.

Intentions: I connect and feel the energy of money and abundance. It feels good. I intend to stay aligned with unconditional love from the highest source of love. I appreciate how love and abundance flow into my life. I expand my mind and creativity to the highest potential. I step into wealth consciousness.

Attachment to a Specific Outcome
In my thirties, my desire was to get married and have a family. When that didn't occur for me at that time I was disappointed and saddened. This sadness was deep within me. I couldn't even imagine not having a child. Years later, I understood that this was not the destiny for my highest good in this lifetime. After going through a challenging period in my late thirties, I gained a new, expanded view on my life. With an expanded scope, I became more accepting of how my life unfolded; trusting that everything happened precisely in the way it was meant to. I was aware that I was learning about self-love and empowerment, and I became tenaciously passionate about providing information for others to empower themselves. This passion became the focus of my life.

If you have attachments and expectations about what you think should be occurring, and it doesn't occur in your desired time frame, in the precise mold you imagined, disappointment could set in. Trust that everything is in divine order, and let it go. You are on your path right now. It may have different turns and outcomes that you are not privy to right now.

Unconditional-Love Beliefs: I am done being a victim of my past hurts and fears and disappointments. I'm at peace with who I am right now. There were no mistakes. I learned many lessons, and I appreciate all the people who came into my life, and the people who are coming into my life. I believe that the universe provides all I ask for and all I need. I understand that there is a higher divine meaning behind all my experiences. I have the wisdom to trust my life path and accept and love myself fully.

Affirmations: I value myself. I feel complete and whole. I trust that everything is in divine order. I *am* powerful. I am power. I am the director and creator of my life. I am loved. I feel accepted and appreciated. I love my life! I am deeply grateful for all the love I have in my life.

Intention: I intend to feel connected to my inner power, and beauty and greatness. I intend to feel the Divine inside me. I choose to drop the "mini script" running in my head about how I wished things were different. I choose to let compassion shine out from my heart. I choose to accept my life fully. I intend to feel powerful and to feel confident in the woman or man I have become and in the life I have right now. I intend to live courageously!

Attachment to Being Liked

As humans, our natural, intrinsic desire is to connect with others on a heart level. These heart connections fill us up and fuel us. But if we are emotionally attached in an unhealthy way, this may be a form of dependency.

I'll share with you a personal story of attachment. About ten years ago, I got a strong feeling to e-mail some information to someone. I did, and a couple of days went by without my getting a response or even a quick thank-you. Whenever I thought about not getting a response, I didn't feel good. It was a small feeling of rejection, of not being liked or valued. On the second day, I was in my bathroom drying my hair, and I had the insight that just the act of my forwarding the information to help this person in some way was a good deed. I didn't need anyone telling me so. I didn't need validation or appreciation. It really didn't matter what the person thought. My intention had been pure. My intention was to pass on this information because it may help. Then I heard inside my head, "I'm a good person, and I don't need anyone telling me so!"

All of a sudden, this song came out of me, and I was singing, dancing around between my bathroom and bedroom, shimmying, hands waving.

> *"I'm a good person, through and through;*
> *I'm a good person, inside out.*
> *I'm a good person, day and night;*
> *I'm a good person all day long!*
> *And I don't need anyone one telling me so!"*
> (This last line is the really loud part of the song.)

Observing Attachments and Processing Emotions

Observe your theme by listening to your own language. When you are personalizing a comment or behavior from someone else and you feel unloved, what are the thoughts in your head? We all have a theme or pattern of how we feel when we personalize. To observe without personalizing, identify the behavior without making it about you. For example, instead of "Hank is really mad at me," change to "Hank is mad." I know, it can be very challenging to lean into the idea that we are not responsible for other people's emotions and choices. We are responsible only for our own energy, actions, and behavior.

During many years as a public speaker and yoga teacher, I've had the opportunity to learn to practice not taking things personally and to truly trust myself. Here's a great, profound lesson I learned early on. When I didn't hear back from at least three people after a talk I made the assumption that they must not have liked it. So I began doubting myself. I should have done more of this or less of that.

A couple of days later, I got this e-mail: "Laurie, your talk was so helpful! Can I buy the DVD?" Another attendee I was wondering about told me she had phone and Internet problems because of a new carrier. She said, "I would love to the purchase the talk and send it to my son." Then another attendee told me how inspiring and helpful I was. This was a huge lesson not to make negative assumptions, not to be self-critical, and to trust and to believe in myself—in short, a lesson in unconditional love. Do you see how ridiculous we can be? Raise your hand and make a commitment to yourself. Say, "I promise to keep my energy to myself, to have the most loving thoughts, to act like my own best friend and be my biggest cheerleader."

Observe your thoughts. Are you telling yourself, "They are rude," or "They don't like me"? Are you feeling unappreciated or rejected? If we are letting others define who we are, letting them control our emotions, then we are living at the mercy of others. We are giving our power away and we are not connected to our wholeness. Anytime we have thoughts such as *they don't like me, she should be more tolerant,* or *how dare he speak to me that way!* It means we care too much about what someone else thinks. When this occurs, we ask ourselves, "Whom am I giving my authority to and why?" We have a belief that is telling us this person has taken value away from us. When we do this we are being conditional with ourselves. It's okay that someone doesn't like us. We can say to ourselves, "Right now they are having this experience of not liking me. I accept that it is real for them. I love me. I like me. And how they feel is their business. What is important to me is how *I* feel about me. With a smile on my face and calm in my heart, I relax in knowing that all is well."

A state of unconditional love is true freedom. You know that you always have choices: the choice to agree or not agree to life situations, freedom to love yourself and not care what anyone thinks. It's up to us to find that place within us that believes anything is possible.

If you feel there is truth to the message the person is sharing with you, think of it as an opportunity to learn something useful. From my experience, if something has a strong charge within me, it's an opportunity to discern that place within me that needs a new perspective, a new belief, or healing.

Unconditional-Love Beliefs: I believe in me. I like me, and that's what's important. I understand that each person is unique, and this includes me. I'm a very valuable person. I deserve to be happy and loved. I trust that I am much more than the drama I'm in now. I believe that I am love, connected to love from above and no one can deplete that within me. I have a knowing that all is well.

Affirmations: I accept the situation just as it is. I'm a good person inside and out. I allow myself to be who I am. I love who I am. I love the feeling of being accepted. I build my inner strength on my own love. The universe loves me unconditionally. I am needed and wanted by the universe. I know that I'm a loving, divine, powerful, infinite, whole being made by unconditional love! My energy is open to friends who are of the highest and purest frequency, who are responsible and reliable. I'm lovable! I am open to my own light! I'm learning how to be my own best friend.

Intentions: I fully accept everything about me. I intend to step out of this drama and remember that all is well. I intend to be my loving self and allow love to flow through me. I intend to feel this love and radiate this love into humanity. I choose to nourish myself with love. I call on,

> connect with, and amplify my light! I bring this state of love consciousness into my being. I choose to connect with my beautiful wholeness inside me. I intend to be happy. I intend to be the source of my own strength. I choose not to allow this person or situation to control my emotions. I choose to stay in peace.

Attachment to Someone Else's Behavior

A friend of mine named Lisa was buying a new car and was told she could get three thousand dollars for her old car. Instead of selling her car, Lisa generously decided to give it to her brother. Lisa was concerned with getting the car out of her name and was having a difficult time getting a response from her brother. As the weeks went by and still no response came, Lisa felt unappreciated by her brother. In fact, she was so angry, she wanted to drive several hours away to take the car back. Finally, she decided to go to her local Department of Motor Vehicles office and sign paperwork declaring the car a gift and taking it out of her name. Lisa and I spoke about this situation. I asked her, "When you gave your car to your brother what was your original intention?" She replied, "I knew my brother was struggling, and I wanted to help him out." I told her, "Stick with your original intention, which was very loving. Feel good about yourself that you could do such a loving act. Don't be concerned how your brother is responding to you. You are not responsible for his reaction—only your own. If he can't offer you gratitude, that's the place he is in right now. It has nothing to do with you. And it doesn't detract from the good deed you did."

How do you know if you are judging someone's behavior? Check in with yourself. What are you saying? Are you annoyed or angry at how someone responded or acted? Do you wish the person would act differently? Are you discussing with others all the things you don't like about this person? Do you want this person to understand that what they said was wrong and affected you? If you answered yes, then this is a clear sign that you have work to do in getting into a space of unconditional acceptance. It's not about pointing the finger at them and trying to change them by telling them all the things you think are wrong about them and focusing on how they behave. It's important to understand that you are the manager of yourself and that your job is to process your disappointment and your emotions. And when you do, you are drawing your power back to yourself. You are putting attention, focus, and action on bringing yourself back to a state of peace. This is unconditional love. You can catch yourself and say, "I accept you, and you are welcome here."

Trust your feelings and tune in to how your body feels. You don't need other people's approval if it's not healthy for you to be around this or that person so much. Does your energy feel alive or drained? It may be time to establish boundaries. Even though you are allowing someone to be exactly who they are, you can choose how much of yourself you give to them, how much time and energy they consume in your mind. Ask yourself, "What is the most unconditional, loving thoughts and actions for myself right now?"

We can't force people to behave in ways that we consider acceptable. But we can choose to be aware of our emotions and process them while we are living life. To be aware of our emotions and not allow them to be our runaway driver, we need to be present in our mind. If our mind is off thinking about the future or stuck in the past, then we are not present.

If you have a pattern of reacting in anger toward specific situations and people, it's a reminder to do your inner work. Discover what beliefs are underneath the anger, and process your emotions. If I find I am personalizing a situation, I find it helpful to ask, "How is this taking away part of me? How is this making me smaller? How is this making me 'less than'?" And if I'm being honest, I have to reply, "It's not." Whether someone returns your calls, returns your love, is angry at you because your dog left a little present on his lawn, it's not your business. It's *their* life stuff. You are still the loving, whole human being you have always been.

The less we personalize and the more we stay in an emotional state of neutrality, not making the story about us,

Observing Attachments and Processing Emotions

the better we can listen and let the external noise bounce off us without our internalizing it. In most cases when we personalize, we are making an assumption about how someone is feeling. I'll give you an example: My boyfriend was away on a trip. He didn't call me for a couple of nights. In my head, I personalized this behavior by assuming he didn't want to speak to me. After he got back I found out he didn't have cell phone service for the first couple of days of his trip.

Taking things personally devalues you, and, of course, this is *conditional* love. This is a common scenario for a person who is not aligned with their own beautiful light. We were taught to look outside ourselves for our emotional compass. But as we awaken we stop doubting ourselves based on other people's behavior or life outcomes. Trust that everything happens perfectly and is in divine order. And that you are amazing! And if someone didn't want to be your friend anymore, there is a divine reason for that, and on the horizon are new friends who are more aligned with who you are. The more fluidly we allow ourselves to flow through our life, the more at ease and empowered we will be.

When we choose a higher perspective this lets compassion enter our heart. And when your heart is filled with compassion you may see the situation differently. You may notice that this person you are angry with is, in fact, reacting from his or her own fears and limitations. This knowledge will help you not to personalize and internalize their behavior.

Unconditional-Love Beliefs: I trust that everything is in divine order. We all live in our own reality, interpreting life through our beliefs and views. I allow other people to be who they are, without allowing their behavior to take anything away from me. My worthiness is independent of others. I have the resources in me to be peaceful. I am learning not to impose my own reality on others, and to understand that another person's reality is the best thing for their own evolutionary process.

Affirmations: I make good decisions. I'm proud of my abilities to draw my energy back to myself. I'm very responsible and kind. I appreciate my loving heart. I receive goodness graciously! I am an infinite, beautiful, powerful, divine being, with everything inside me that I need to be happy. I'm grateful for my life. I am healing and awakening.

Intentions: I intend to take action in a positive direction. I let go of any animosity and bad feelings. I choose not to complain; instead, I choose to be proactive. I choose to embrace the positive aspects! I anchor all my relationships in love and light. I intend to be my fullest potential in all ways. I disconnect and remove all energies that don't serve my highest good.

Attachment in a Business Relationship

In my past, I was in a business relationship in which I felt I was being taken advantage of. I was afraid to say no and set appropriate boundaries. I felt I wasn't good enough to do it on my own. I felt I "needed" those business associates. I was attached to the notion that I needed their support, instead of appreciating my own abilities and believing in my own path. This situation helped me do so. It helped me value myself.

When we are hurt by someone's behavior toward us, we are personalizing the behavior. Our ego comes forth. We get angry, run away, or want to hurt them back. We then judge them as being wrong—insensitive, controlling, manipulative, pushy, abrasive—and we point out all the things they do that are wrong. We project our pain onto them. And then we take it one step further and tell them they need to learn to be different from the way they are now. If we make them wrong, it makes us feel better. When you are with a person who is pushy, controlling, or manipulative this is a great opportunity to practice saying what you really mean and stating what will work for you.

Look at your anger. Look at where you put blame. Ask, "What is my perception? What is my mini story about this situation? Can I change my story? Can I stop listing all the things wrong about this person and how they mistreated me and how they should behave? Can I switch my focus to processing my own emotions and completely accept who they are right now?"

Humanity needs more love! Most people are starving for unconditional love. How can you be more loving to yourself? Each of us perceives life through our own life filters. And we project our life issues onto others.

Our responsibility is to process our fears, hurts, sadness, and insecurities. Being the manager of our emotional state is an act of self-love. During this process, we are loving and kind. Allow and embrace your feelings. Love them. Give yourself the time you need to mourn the loss of your business relationship.

There are many times when situations occur unexpectedly and our energy system is triggered. We may be caught off guard and may be unsure how to respond. And in this case, the situation may feel somewhat traumatic. In this type of scenario, I have learned to respond this way: "I'm not feeling comfortable right now, and it would feel better for me if you would please _____."

Unconditional-Love Beliefs: Even though I have this sadness right now, I do believe and trust that this occurred for a divine reason. I trust that the information will unfold and that I will have clarity. I know that each person is doing the best they can with the tools they have today, with their level of conscious awareness. I don't personalize their behavior or choices. I'm not responsible for another person's emotions. I accept them right where they are, and I don't judge. My worth and self-esteem derive from *me*—from how I feel about myself. I understand that people see life through their experiences. A person cannot see anything that they can't feel in their own heart. I can give unconditional love without an attachment to receiving anything back. My interaction with this person is a gift to me and is helping me grow. I have the resources and talents to succeed.

Affirmations: The universe is a friendly place. I accept this moment with complete ease. I am pure, bright light and love. I'm a fully empowered being. I step into my sovereignty. I'm at peace with the way I responded. I know who I am. I love my heart. And that is enough. I'm a wonderful person.

Intentions: I intend to stay emotionally neutral and centered. I intend to feel peace in my heart and support from above. I choose to focus on the positive aspects of my experiences. I intend to approach my life with a high state of consciousness. I connect with the frequencies of trust, empowerment, and love. I allow my heart to navigate me toward things and experiences that feel good. I feel forgiveness and full acceptance for others and myself. I am releasing the emotional attachment to _____'s behavior. I disconnect the energies. I remove myself from the drama and say good bye. I step out of the drama into the bigger picture of my life. This higher perspective says, "I'm learning how to keep my energy within myself, how to stay grounded, create boundaries, use my voice, and build a stronger connection to self. I choose to thrive."

Attachment to a Friend

I would like to offer you a belief of mine. When a relationship changes structure and people go their separate ways, I believe that these two people are done learning and growing together. It may not feel good, but it may be for the highest good. It's not necessary for your personal evolution any longer. This change may be clearing your path. And when you believe this, it takes the personalization out of the equation. Nothing is wrong. And actually, it's in divine order. If one person gets the feeling or intuition to move on and go in another direction, it means their soul lesson was learned. They may have new desires and needs that the current relationship doesn't support. The love is still there and doesn't go away. Some relationships part ways for a time and then come back together. During the time apart, they were meant to learn separately from each other. Trust that everything is unfolding perfectly.

On a beautiful early-morning walk, a thought popped into my head—an observation that a particular friend hadn't been e-mailing and calling me as much as she had in the past. I felt a familiar sadness in my heart. It felt like the old theme of "She doesn't want to be my friend anymore." I felt that I was losing love. I recalled having a dream the night before, in which a similar theme played out. A friend in the dream didn't want to be my friend anymore, and I was sad. This was showing me precisely the belief and fear within me that needed to be healed. It's no coincidence that I had that dream the night before and remembered the feeling I had in the dream.

Why did I jump directly to a sense of loss, to believing that something must be wrong with me? I still had residue left from childhood, believing *they don't like me,* and *they don't want to be my friend. Why does it always have to be that something is wrong?* A lightbulb went off. I had the thought *well, maybe I can talk to her.* But that thought didn't feel good. And then I saw the image of trying to squeeze water from a rock. You can squeeze all you want, but you'll be wasting your time. Then the intuitive thought came to me: *What if I'm moving toward something? What if my energy is attracting a deeper, more authentic friendship? What if all I need to do to feel better is to ACCEPT our relationship just as it is, without wanting anything to be different or labeling it as "wrong" or making myself feel not wanted?* Soon after I transitioned into a place of peace, my friend contacted me. I asked her if there was anything wrong because I haven't heard from her. She shared with me her story of what she was going through which had nothing to do with me.

Enjoy your life exactly how it is. Fighting "what is" creates the resistance and sadness. Before making assumptions ask questions.

Relationships with people change. Some of our relationships may last, and some may change form. We all have had friends enter our lives and leave, as we have done the same for others. Love does not die. If a friend stops being your friend and you are sad and wondering what is wrong with you, try to see a higher perspective that looks like this: "We were meant to share our lives together for that time. I enjoyed many experiences and have learned many things, too. I bless him/her. They are amazing in many ways, and so am I. I trust that new, loving, like-minded friends are on the horizon, and I'm excited to share life with them. I trust exactly how my life is unfolding right now. I accept life as it is, completely, right now. My life is moving forward."

If you find that you are lonely, acknowledge and thank your emotions for alerting you that you are ready to open up to more love in your life, or a deeper connection with life and with yourself. Look at this emotion of "loneliness" as an opportunity to say, "Thank you for telling me that I'm ready to connect deeper within and with the world. I'm open to ways to express my creativity and feel more fulfilled. I'm ready to feel connected. I'm open to a deeper and more expansive reach in the world. I'm ready to have a greater connection to all there is, to feel more alive, and to feel more love and passion. I open myself to love within and all around me. I open myself to more experiences to express and be love."

KNOW THAT YOU DESERVE TO BE HONORED. You deserve friends who honor you. You deserve clients, customers, coworkers, employers who respect you. How are you not honoring yourself? Say, "I deserve to be honored for the divine, beautiful being that I am. I honor myself."

Unconditional-Love Beliefs: I accept this situation. I have no expectations. I believe that I can release my blame and anger and move into faith and trust! I am grateful for the opportunity to speak up for myself. My friend really helped me find my voice. I will miss the good times we did share. I trust that new friends are entering my life and that the relationships will be respectful, with a healthy, equitable exchange of support and love. I had the opportunity to share love, be vulnerable, and use my voice. I'm grateful for the life experience we shared together. I believe that my sadness is temporary and that everything happens for a reason. I have respect for them. I respect myself.

Affirmations: I am a lovable person and a great friend. I am worthy of unconditional love and heart connections. I'm my own best friend. I am a wonderful, divine, infinite being. I really do value who I am right now, and trust that everything is in divine order. Love is all around me and in me. I'm one with all there is.

Intentions: I ask and intend for the Divine's unconditional love and peace to flow through me, inside every cell of my body. I breathe in love. I choose to validate myself and not allow another person's choices to affect my worthiness. I intend to make wonderful new, loving friendships with like-minded people. I send good wishes to all the friends who have been in my life, and I open up and welcome mutually beneficial new friends. I make room for peace! I intend to focus on creating a deeper and more loving connection with myself. I choose to make my well-being a priority.

Attachment to Not Being Rejected

Fear of being rejected can secretly hold us back in many different areas of life. I realized that I had a fear of rejection and wasn't even conscious of it. I was perusing someone's web site and resonating with her speaking style and material. I had the thought to reach out and make a business connection with her. As I was looking at the books on her recommended list this thought popped in: *she's not going to be interested in my work*. In that moment, I was making this person better than me because she had a PhD and other titles, and I was not valuing myself.

This was an indication that I needed to process feelings of rejection within me. I allowed it to speak to me, and what I uncovered was a variety of areas in my life where I felt rejected, and then, underneath that, I discovered a layer of sadness. I processed the sadness and transmuted it into unconditional love. My fear of being rejected stemmed from a sense of unworthiness. It also showed me where I was being conditional with myself. You can't have unconditional love for yourself and be fearful of being rejected at the same time. I actually allowed this fear to stop me from doing something that would have been a positive, supportive and loving action.

In my meditation, the intuitive message I received was, "This is the time to really trust—to really dig deep and trust everything about you. This is a message about trust."

I also did a few rounds of meridian tapping on specific acupuncture points to allow the brain to connect with the emotion of rejection in my body. I took a few deep breaths, in through my nose and out through my mouth.

Review different areas of your life where you have a feeling of being rejected. It can be very subtle. Say you bring a huge basket of clothes to a resale shop, and they purchase only one thing. You walk away feeling bad, taking it personally that they didn't want any more of your clothes. You feel rejected.

Notice the different areas where you don't allow yourself to be vulnerable or where you display a lack of courage. What is holding you back? And listen to your stories and excuses. Then ask, "If there were no fear of being rejected by anyone, how would I proceed? How would I express myself? What actions would I take?"

Unconditional-Love Beliefs: I believe that it is healthy to process my fear of rejection. I love how honest and present I am with myself. It's exciting and empowering to process my emotions. I have a lot to offer! I know it's not personal. It's not even my business. I choose not to reject myself. I know that what I am experiencing is what is most helpful for my soul's evolution. I have the courage to live each day as if it were my last. This situation is a tiny drop in my book of life and it soon will pass. I trust that everything is in divine order. I have the resources to create a beautiful path—one filled with joy, love, and great happiness!

Affirmations: I appreciate that I am able to discern insecurities within me. I'm awesome! I'm needed! I'm courageous. I'm a beautiful person! I love you, _____ [insert your name]. I'm whole.

Intentions: I allow myself to be vulnerable. I move forward in my life, with courage, patience and an open heart. I trust that I'm on my divine path and that it is very needed and purposeful. I intend to stay centered within my own personal empowerment. I stand strong in my beautiful radiance.

Attachment to How We Want to Be Perceived

This seductive trap hooks us into how we want to be perceived by others. And we are caught when we don't allow our true self to come forward. We may be putting on a little act to try to come across in a specific way or look a particular way by playacting a particular role. And at times, we aren't even aware that we're doing it.

A woman I knew had a strong attachment to being seen as rich. In her mind, she attached her sense of self to the prestige of material wealth. In conversations with people, she went on at length about the homes she owned, her investments, her high-end cars, and famous people she knew. How we behave is a clear indication of our own inner perception. *And it's liberating to trust that you are enough right now, being you, without the need for others to see you in a particular, controlled view. Our behavior places a magnifying mirror on our insecurities. If we are playing a role to be perceived in a specific way, it places a big neon sign on the insecurity, saying, "I don't love myself just as I am. I feel inadequate in some way." Looking on from outside, it's as obvious as an elephant in the room.*

If you find you are caring too much about what others think, you are giving your power away. You have walked away from yourself. So walk back and be comfortable just being your beautiful, authentic self without any expectation.

I have found this attachment to be true in other scenarios, such as wanting a parent's approval. Someone will act in a particular way, follow a particular career path, espouse particular politics or follow a particular faith, live in a particular city, or even marry a particular partner—all just to be perceived as a perfect child.

Unconditional-Love Beliefs: Being me is enough. I was made on purpose, from the highest source of love, just the way I am. I love and trust myself. I trust that being authentic and real is safe and comfortable. I choose to be me over any fear. I choose to live my life being real. If someone doesn't like who I am, that is not my concern. I love being around authentic, genuine people!

Affirmations: I'm eternally grateful to the Divine for creating me. I embrace and accept myself exactly how I am right now. I have heaven inside my heart. I'm pure unconditional love, joy, eternal and infinite, divine intelligence. I'm one with all of consciousness.

Intentions: I intend to be connected to my truth, feel joy, and be grateful to everyone and everything. I keep my energy and focus within me. I allow my light to shine! I feel freedom in my heart. I connect to my wisdom, my gifts, and my abilities. I intend to stand strong in my beautiful light! I share myself authentically and honestly in all my relationships.

Attachment to Pleasing People

I had a coaching client who was more concerned with saying and responding in a way he thought I wanted him to respond than with expressing the way he really felt. And when he didn't follow up on the goals that he had set for himself he thought I was going to be disappointed, and was afraid to face me. He was attached to what I thought of him—attached to pleasing me. He was afraid that he had let me down, and that meant he had failed. We are not going to please everyone, and it's too stressful to take responsibility for other people's emotions. We owe it to ourselves to be our own best friend and be congruent with ourselves.

Look within your life. Is there an area where you take a particular action because you are afraid someone will be mad at you if you don't? Do you agree to certain things because you want to please others? Do you agree with the group because you want to fit in? Are you afraid of not being liked? Are you afraid that others may get angry with you? Are you afraid love will walk away from you? How can you give yourself what you need? If you answered yes to any of the above questions, do the "Exercise for Processing Emotions" visualization at the end of this chapter.

Unconditional-Love Beliefs: I am worthy of loving and kind relationships. I embrace all of me completely. How someone perceives me is their business, and how I perceive myself is mine. I'm free just to be me, real and authentic. My voice is important. I believe that when I'm honest and authentic I am powerful! I'm responsible for acting in a loving manner toward others and myself and for expressing myself in an authentic way. I'm a human, and at times, I need to give myself a break. I do the best I can, and I love that about me. I believe that when the energy between people is clear, honest, and clean this minimizes expectations or assumptions. I have the inner strength and love to move past this situation.

Affirmations: I deeply and completely love and accept every part of myself. I'm an equal to all that I meet. I'm safe. Many people love me. My unique essence creates a beautiful ripple effect in our universe. I allow my light to shine brightly! I step into my sovereignty, and it feels good! I'm strong.

Intentions: I intend to be honest, kind, and up front. I take steps to practice being completely authentic and to move through my insecurities in peace. I step into my sovereignty, and it feels good!

Attachment to Knowing What Lies Ahead in Life

I can remember speaking to a client who felt that she had no way out of her unhappy relationship. She met everything I suggested with her reasons why she needed to stay in the relationship. Her responses showed me that she was not yet ready to take action and move in another direction.

Letting go of what she was comfortable with, with what she knew, was too scary. She found not knowing what the future held simply too scary. Her fear of the unknown kept her a victim, a prisoner to her current situation. But over time, it became more detrimental to her spirit to stay where she was, so she began to explore her options. This can be a very painful internal struggle.

I have experienced this struggle of being in just such an intense, fearful state. If you find yourself in this state, the key is to try to let go and not hold on so tightly. Continue to bring yourself back to the present moment and focus on what you do know, and live one day at a time, trusting your divine life path. Embrace each moment with peace and acceptance, and trust that clarity will come. We are not always meant to see the completely finished puzzle with all the differently shaped pieces put together just so. We are meant to live one moment at a time, flowing gracefully down the current. And if we get stuck and can't find the next puzzle piece, we slow down, take our time, and pray for support to stay on our highest path and ask for reassurance. We meditate and listen to our intuition. We ask for divine clarity and direction so that we may open our eyes, expand our view, and observe our thoughts and intentions. And, then we follow our intuition, take the appropriate action, and observe what is showing up and how the universe is supporting us. Before you know it, you are onto the next puzzle piece!

Unconditional-Love Beliefs: I believe I am exactly where I am meant to be right now. I understand that there is much more to the bigger picture than I comprehend right now, but that things will unfold. I trust that the information I do know is what I'm meant to know at this time. I have within me everything I need to be happy, healthy, and whole. I trust my life's path, my intuition. I trust my heart, and I trust myself to have the courage to navigate my way to healthier experiences and opportunities. I am worthy of attaining my goals. I believe I will receive the exact help and information when the time is right. My positive intentions and thoughts are manifesting in my life. And all is coming together in perfect timing. I have the patience and the time to live my life peacefully in the present moment.

Affirmations: I am a wise, divine being, energetically connected to everything and everyone. I embrace and accept all my emotions without any judgment. I am comfortable and at peace, living in the moment! I trust that this is a beautiful, abundant, and friendly universe. I'm okay right now. I have the courage to feel empowered, and I believe that I can live one day at a time, one moment at a time, and feel safe. I know that all the puzzle pieces come together at the right time. I trust this to be true! I am powerful. I am power.

Intentions: I intend to live in harmony and be happy right now. I intend to be a witness to my emotions, to listen to them and let them express, and to bring divine light and love to them. I intend also to interrupt my thinking and ask myself, "What is the best and highest thought I can have right now?" I ask and intend for my loving angels to send me calming energy and stay by my side. I ask and intend to hear my higher wisdom. I intend to follow my heart, stay fully in the moment, and create a new beginning. I intend to have faith and trust my life. I'm committed to living in a space of unconditional love!

Detaching

The fewer emotional attachments we have, the freer and more empowered we are as humans. It can take time and practice not to identify, not to personalize, and instead to become objective, neutral, the witness and the observer, without making someone or something bad or good, wrong or right. You are just observing without classifying. During a stressful time, remind yourself that you are much more than this experience and that this experience will pass. It is just one drop of water in your entire sphere of existence.

Detachment allows us to keep our energy peaceful within ourselves. In a state of detachment, we are grounded in the knowledge of who we are and in our power. We are in our divine eternal connection with love from above, and in our understanding of divine orchestration. And, we are adaptable and flexible during our life circumstances. This is an expression of unconditional love!

It can be tricky. Even for me, as I was in the process of writing this book about getting free from emotional attachment, I had the awareness that I was too emotionally attached to the outcome. I needed to let go and trust the creative process. Our relationships are a mirror of ourselves. They are reflecting back to us what is stored in our consciousness.

If you find you are too emotionally invested in something or someone, bring yourself back to reminding yourself of the beautiful, fully empowered, infinite being that you are. Place your hand on your heart, close your eyes, breathe and say, "I release and disconnect from all attachments, worries and concerns. My home is within myself. I am free." You are not defined by any particular emotion. Your pure essence is always unconditional love.

Take-Away Exercise for Processing Emotions

Visualization

Sit down and close your eyes. Place one hand on your belly, and the other hand on your heart. Breathe in through your nose and out through your mouth. Relax all your muscles. Feel the rise and fall of your belly and heart, moving with your breath. Tune into your heart. How does your heart feel right now? What emotions are you feeling or sensing? Acknowledge the anger, resentment, fear, sadness, disappointment, insecurity, or whatever you're feeling. What does it look like or feel like? Say, "I feel; I allow." Allow yourself to feel the emotion fully. Don't feel bad or guilty for having a fear or for being angry. Simply allow it to be present.

Where is the sensation inside your body? Does your emotion have a color or texture? Just notice what it looks like. Now inform the emotion that it is welcome here. Ask the fear, sadness, rejection, or anger if there is anything this energy would like to say to you. Listen and trust what you sense and intuit. Allow the emotion to fully express as big and loud as it wants. Observe it without analyzing. If there are fears ask yourself the reasons why you want to keep these fears. When you feel that the emotion is done sharing, say, "Thank you for sharing. I love you." Send love to the emotion. Take a breath. Now say, "I am ready to release this emotion that says, '_____,' [fill in the blank] because I intend to heal, connect to my wholeness, let it go, and take back my power. Thank you for allowing me to observe and listen to you."

Now take a big breath and allow the emotion(s) to go free back into oneness, back to the Divine. Breathe love and light into your body, into the areas that we once filled by the emotions, for several minutes or until you begin to feel better. Say, "I raise my body's vibration and place into my cells the essence of joy, trust, love, and light. I reprogram the cells to believe in myself and in my dreams. I am aware of my divine DNA that knows the truth of who I am. I choose to remember that I am love." In your own time, open your eyes, wiggle your fingers and toes, and stretch your arms up over your head.

Write this in your journal and read it out loud: "I replace this energy with greater love, greater connection to my own divinity, deeper self-trust, and an abundance of inner strength." (Continue adding whatever qualities you wish to replace the old energies with.) Then say, "I am deeply, eternally grateful for this love and support from above!"

The next step is to write down this situation as if it is resolved. What would your life be like without that fear? How would someone who loves themselves perceive your situation? How does that make you feel? What are your new feelings? Write this story out in your journal. Now is a good time to change your activity. What have you done in the past that has brought you from conflict to peace? It may be a walk with a neighbor, a good chat with a best friend, walking or romping with your dog, baking, helping someone else, doing a spontaneous act of kindness, playing with a baby, watching a movie, dancing, singing, painting, or reading a fun novel.

(Part of the above process was inspired by Inelia Benz's fear processing exercise at www.ascension101.com)

3

UNCONDITIONAL ACCEPTANCE AND FORGIVENESS: NO MORE JUDGMENT

It's time to love and accept yourself unconditionally, no matter what. You are willing to embrace, love, and acknowledge all parts of who you are in the moment—even in those moments when you are not feeling good, looking good, or even "being good." To feel peaceful, we must accept our life, past and present. We must accept others and ourselves. Acceptance is allowing things to be as they are, surrendering to the flow of life. And with this surrendering, we express a healthy dose of adaptability and flexibility. Many of us have been raised to compare ourselves to others and to find fault in others and ourselves. We project our own ideas, attitudes, beliefs and feelings onto others. These projections come from our own personal life experiences, which form the basis of our own insecurities and fears. But now, we are making choices based on preference, without the need to make anyone or anything wrong or "bad." We can allow others to be who they are, yet choose a path that has a natural resonance and natural draw for us. We move out of blame and judgment into forgiveness, compassion, and full acceptance.

Acceptance of Self

As we evolve, we place a strong value on being in our heart center, trusting our feelings, reconnecting to the wholeness and resourcefulness within us. You move gracefully through your life, with the absolute *knowing* that everything is in divine order. We value our gifts and what we bring to the world, knowing that our gifts are just as valuable as anyone else's. And we understand that the Divine values everyone equally, no matter their job title, gender, skin color, age, tax bracket, or religion.

During one of my beautiful morning walks, I was in deep contemplation and received a very strong intuitive message. The vision I received resembled a mini movie of how all my thoughts about "not being good enough" played out in all the areas of my life. I could feel the emotions that I felt in each scenario. I realized how hard on myself I was for most of my life: I was not pretty enough, not smart enough, not skinny enough, not wise enough. The question popped into my mind: *Are you ever going to feel good enough? You spent four decades feeling this way. Do you really want to spend another four?* I felt sad. But instead of pushing the sadness away, I just let it be there. I embraced it and welcomed it. I said, "I love you." I asked the sadness if there was anything it wanted to share. The sadness was done speaking to me. It was ready to be transmuted to love. I forgave myself. I said, "I'm so sorry for treating you like this, for comparing you to others, and for all the ways I made you feel inept. I'm really sorry! Please forgive me." I was finally ready to take back my power and accept me just as I was. And you can do it, too. As different situations come up for you discern your feelings: feelings of jealousy, ineptness, insecurity, shame, or envy. These feelings are a sign that somewhere you don't feel good enough.

Do you believe that you, as a divine being, are enough right now? You don't have to *become* someone; you are someone *right now*. You are unique, and you have a unique gift to share with the world. From a place of full acceptance, you are not at the mercy of others. You don't need someone or something else to make you feel good enough. You don't need to justify or prove your value. As we live in a space of full acceptance, we move away from focusing on who we are not, who we wish to be, and how things and others should be. There's a word for all that: it's called "judgment." Do you feel that getting this or that degree, romantic partner, amount of money, job or marital title, or degree of fame would allow you to feel a specific yearned-for emotion such as happiness, love, success, or acceptance? The thing is, everything is already *right* with you. You understand that you are a divine being made in perfection! And you have a choice of how you want to experience life here on earth. Say, "Everything is right with me just as I am right now." Take a deep belly breath. I lived with self-doubt for many years, and it's a feeling of always being behind. It's time you valued yourself right now as a beautiful, magical light that is beaming love.

Many of us have been hurt during our life, and many of us have created a belief system, based in fear, that says "people hurt me." Well, what if it's time to let go of all that pain? What if we are being asked to release all the old limitations and step into a new place within us? And this new place within says, "I love you so-o-o-o much! I've got your back. No need to be afraid and build up all this aloofness to protect yourself. Just stand tall and shine your bright light. You are healed now. You are now living in a higher frequency. You don't need all that restraining emotional protection anymore. It's time just to be, to love, to accept."

I have learned that being authentic is self-love. In fact, it is the ultimate act of empowering and accepting oneself. I had a client who was contemplating separating from his wife. He had spent several years pretending in many ways, to be someone he wasn't, to please everyone around him. He was not honoring his authentic self. When he did decide it was time to make a change he began an inner journey to become very real with himself and live in an authentic way. He unconditionally accepted himself.

Accept what is occurring. To be in full acceptance of this moment right now, place your focus on all your senses, with your full attention. Are you fully in the moment right now, while you are reading these words on this page? How are you feeling right now? How does your body feel? If you are resting on a chair or couch, how does it feel? Are you relaxed? What sounds are around you? What smells are around you?

Unconditional Acceptance and Forgiveness: No More Judgment

What do you see around you? Do you accept this moment fully? What is your inner guidance whispering to you? Say, "I fully accept this moment."

Many times, our mind worries about all the things we *don't know*. If you are frustrated because you're unclear about your life's purpose or how to move forward, accept that you don't know everything right now. Don't resist what is happening. Don't even resist *not knowing* what is happening. Say, "It's okay that I don't know everything right now. I trust that my life unfolds perfectly and that I gain clarity everyday. I keep my focus on what I do know, and build from there. I ask and intend to draw to me clear signs to guide me on my path, for my highest good. I ask to remove any emotional blocks that stand in my way. I ask to be in peace in this moment."

How do we know when we are demonstrating full acceptance of self? I believe that it is happening when we can say, "I like me. I accept my past. I do the best I can. My mistakes are reference points that help me be open to new perspectives." And with a sincere smile, we say, "I have a lot of wonderful reference points." Close your eyes, breathe, and relax. Say, "I am filled with love, filled with light, and filled with the new energies that are supporting my soul's growth. I choose to accept whatever is presented, with love and grace. I choose to *upgrade* my mind's and my body's response to life! I choose a positive attitude that *knows* and *trusts* that all is well and that everything is happening for my best and highest good. I feel supported in all ways." Take a belly breath and relax.

> "To be beautiful means to be yourself. You don't need to be accepted by others. You need to accept yourself."
>
> —Thich Nhat Hanh

A yoga student shared with me that she thought if she accepted herself fully, it meant she would become complacent. I explained to her that from my point of view, self-acceptance and complacence are two different things. I accept who I am, fully, right now, and allow myself to move toward my goals and desires. To accept yourself fully means you accept everything in the present moment, without any resistance, criticism, or judgment. You accept *what is*, because if you didn't, you would cause unnecessary stress. Each of us is innately prewired with specific desires and individual avenues of creative expression. We naturally move in the direction of our heart's desires.

Acceptance of Your Past

To be in full acceptance, we understand that it's a waste of time and energy to wish our past were different or to hold on to our past. As a powerful and responsible person, I accept my choices, learn from them, and make the appropriate changes that are in alignment with my divine self. We understand that the person we were then made those choices based on our level of self-love and personal empowerment. *Our mistakes* are showing us what we do not resonate with. And this gives us a new awareness. You don't have to have critical or shaming thoughts. You don't have to condemn yourself. That is *conditional* love. Full acceptance of what occurred is unconditional love.

A friend of mine shared with me that she was upset that she didn't go to college. She was holding on to a combination of regret, feeling unworthy, and disappointment and anger toward her parents. Even though she is happily married, has a beautiful family of her own, and raised her children, she lives with this bundle of remorse. My friend is not alone. Many people regret choices they made in the past. And if we can recognize that who we were in the past was exactly who we were meant to be, we can then set ourselves free. What if everything is in divine order? What if, in this lifetime, you are and always have been on your life path and have been divinely directed according to your blueprint for your evolution? Are you willing to forgive yourself and let it go?

In every moment, we make choices based on our knowledge, mind-set, and consciousness at the time. Mastery of our energy is of key importance. We become acutely aware of our emotions. We process, transmute, and release what is draining us or disturbing us—baggage such as wishing for a different past. We can't change what occurred. But, we *can* make peace with it, learn from it, and use what we learned to make better decisions for our present and future. To learn the most from our experiences, we can ask questions. *What was the main lesson I learned during that period in my life? What action steps did I take that brought me to a healthier place?*

The most productive way to use our energy is to focus on positive solutions and unlimited possibilities that are aligned with our heart and intuition. You can hold on to your bad feelings, or you can forgive yourself because you deserve inner peace. Be willing to say, "It's okay that I let go and surrender my angst, my struggles, and my disappointments. I release and let go once and for all! I unconditionally accept myself right now! I choose to be grounded within my own beautiful light." The difference between holding on to the past and learning about self-love is that your energy now supports unconditional love, gently pushing you into your sovereignty. You are being asked to live connected to your heart, live authentically, and love who you are as a powerful and beautiful divine being.

Upgrading Your Definition of Who You Are

I had the epiphany that I needed to upgrade my definition of myself. I noticed that when thinking of myself as a younger person, I was still remembering myself with the memory of my old pain and insecurities. If you do the same thing, remind yourself that you can expand your vision by allowing the 10-year-old, 18-year-old, or 49-year-old you to be at peace now. All your experiences brought you to who you are right now. It's time to integrate the healed, empowered, and sovereign present-time you into your past images of yourself. Imagine yourself healed at every age, by viewing the younger you with a heart full of love. Allow gratitude to flow through you for all the courage it took to make it through all your past challenges. Be grateful to yourself for having the wisdom to heal your wounds, and the courage to forge ahead and be the openhearted person you are today. See the younger you receiving and feeling your praise, gratitude, love, and applause. Let it fill every cell of your being. Create a new image of a brave, courageous, and wise younger you. You took the bumps in the road and learned how to love yourself. You did your job beautifully and perfectly.

Say, "I love myself. I love the person I was when I was younger. I accept all the choices, past behaviors, and perceptions I made in my life. I'm a lovable soul! I understand that I did the best I could with the tools I had and with my level of consciousness at the time. I bless the person I was then. I did an awesome job getting me to where I am today. I intend to live fully in the present moment, in full acceptance of my entire life."

And even now do you need to upgrade your current definition of yourself? If so, say, "I ask to feel my wholeness. I ask to expand my consciousness into a higher, more expanded view of myself—one that acknowledges my infiniteness, divinity, and beauty. Please help me see myself from the highest perspective and see all possibilities for me in all areas of my life."

Unconditional Acceptance: No More Comparisons

I believe that before we were born we were involved in carefully planning out many aspects of our earthly life. We chose our body, major goals to achieve, family and environment, and specific experiences. These choices were made with precision to help us achieve our earthly life's mission.

With this in mind, any self-comparison to others is just a waste of time and energy. You have your own very precise blueprint for your life.

I realized that whenever I am jealous of someone or put someone on a pedestal my feelings of inadequacy are showing me that I have disconnected from myself. When I'm feeling this way it's an instant reminder to reconnect, to plug into my divinity and discern whether there is a place within me that needs healing. If you think you aren't smart enough or aren't as smart as other people, stop and think about this for a minute. Ask yourself, "Who are you giving and projecting your authority and power to?" It's very simple: you were meant to be *you*. You are beneath no one! The most loving way to feel is to understand that you are exactly how you are meant to be. You are a perfect, radiant light being right now! You are whole, you are enough, and you have everything inside you! You are *powerful*! You are light. You are pure consciousness! Say, "I own my own power and authority! I'm an equal to everyone and I live in an infinite reality. I am a beautiful, divine, unique signature that sings my own song and dances my own perfect dance to life. I accept my position and role here on earth!" Remind yourself that in this game here on earth, it's humans who place such an important value on external beauty. Make an agreement to value *inner* beauty.

> *"You are not just a drop in the ocean but also the mighty ocean in the drop."*
>
> —Rumi

Unconditional Acceptance: No More Self-Judgment

To build steadfast inner peace, we spend time exploring our inner world as the witness—observing and watching. The road to acceptance is to let whatever happens occur, and to *just be* instead of labeling life situations as good or bad. It isn't the least bit helpful to think, *I'm such an idiot,* or *because this occurred, I'm not good enough.* That's why we are learning to lighten up, both on others and on ourselves. *Judgment can't live in a space of unconditional love. Say, "I accept myself right now. I'm grateful for many things and for the many people who have blessed my life. I love the perfect picture that I created, and I love all involved in it. I agree to be kinder to myself!"*

A coaching client of mine was having a difficult time understanding the difference between self-criticism and self-acceptance. She felt she couldn't accept behavior of hers that she didn't like, and berated herself regularly. If her house was dusty, she was a bad person. If she gained a few pounds, she was ugly. If she wore a black shirt, she was hiding. During an outdoor jog, if she walked more than she ran, she was lazy. I explained to her that she had options for how to view her experience. A loving perspective is, "Well, I'm proud that I took the time out of my busy day to begin a new routine and walk and run for half an hour. I felt winded, but I know that the more I get out there regularly, the better I will feel. I feel better that I got some exercise!"

In her world, she set herself up to fail. She condemned herself for just about everything. I explained that it's very hard to move forward when we don't accept the present. In my eyes, this beautiful woman is an amazing, smart human being with much to offer the world.

Interestingly, I had two people show up in my world with an "I can't" mentality, and neither of them was conscious of it. The first client I will call Lisa. She was expressing her anxiety at the thought of going to her computer. It's a common thing—many of us can feel anxious or intimidated by a new challenge. At that moment, her energy was not open to any other perspective, and her strong resistance continued in response to several things I mentioned. Then finally, I expressed to her that she had blocks of resistance and was stuck in "I can't." She had a huge "A ha!" moment. She told me her son frequently said, "I can't," and she saw how her son was a reflection of herself. Now she was really motivated to be aware of her limiting statements.

Lisa and I created a quick, easy exercise for her to do if her anxiety sprang up. I suggested that she take a step away from her computer, close her eyes, breathe deeply, and relax. I asked her to connect with her heart, connect with love from above, and say, "*I accept this moment with ease, peace, and openness.*" In the short time I had worked with her, I saw the light inside her turn on, and this radiant, more confident woman emerge. She was stepping into her sovereignty.

The second person was a woman who expressed to me her reasons why she couldn't forgive herself. She felt that she had suffered with a lack of self-love her entire life. And she was not open to trying or hearing anything new. In her mind, she was trapped inside the box of "I can't."

Unconditional Acceptance and Forgiveness: No More Judgment

When was the last time you spent a while fully accepting yourself? Are there any areas of your life where you can move into "I can!"? How often during your day do you focus on your strengths versus your weaknesses? How much time do you give your critical voice to speak and share with you? When the critical voice is saying, "You aren't good enough; you failed; look at all those misspelled words; you're an idiot and a klutz," say, "Thank you for sharing." When your mind begins listing all the things you did wrong and just generally creating self-doubt, say, "Thank you for sharing." Take a breath and then connect with your heart, your higher wisdom, from a place of love. What is the message now? Question your defeatist thoughts. Give your higher wisdom, the heart space, more "airtime." It's imperative that we be mindful of which voice is ruling our inner world. Say, "I choose to allow my higher self and heart more airtime."

We attune ourselves with precision to hear the voice of our higher self and grab on to these messages. The messages that your higher self whispers to you are loving and wise. In quiet contemplation, you can hear or sense messages such as "You're going to be okay; trust what you are doing; this is going to be a great year." In the higher realms of the universe, there is no judgment.

Can you say, "I love my insecurities"? This is part of accepting all parts of you. If you feel resistance in your body when you say that statement, locate that energy block in your body and process it. Admire your own qualities. Be on the lookout for feeling your own inner strength. Say, "I intend to feel my own strength and beauty! I accept my wisdom and intuitive abilities." You carry powerful energy of brilliance and beauty within you; it's part of your original makeup. Your true essence of unconditional love is always with you. It may just be covered up by hurt from the past—disappointments, insecurities, and fears—but it's still there. The value of who you are is immeasurable.

Unconditional Acceptance: No More Personalizing

A yoga student of mine suddenly stopped attending class. I was concerned about him because he had some medical issues. About a month or so later, he called me on the phone and told me he was attending another yoga class. At that time, he didn't share any other explanation. For a couple of weeks, I took it personally, feeling that he had left my class because he didn't like it. Roughly six months went by, and out of the blue, he walked back into yoga class. At the end of class, he approached me and said, "I went to the other class because my friends were taking it and convinced me to join them." I had no idea that was why he had stopped coming.

This story exemplifies why taking other people's actions and behavior personally is a waste of time and energy. I was grateful that the universe showed me the truth and taught me to accept life situations with peace and to trust that everything is perfect. It really isn't my business what someone chooses. My business is to stay in a space of unconditional love for self by accepting life without personalizing or making assumptions.

Throughout your day, try to be aware of when you are personalizing someone else's actions. Pay attention to your emotions especially if you are really upset or angry. This may be an indication that you are taking a situation personally. And if you are, ask yourself, "Why do I feel that what they say or do has anything to do with me?" What part of you feels inadequate or unloved or not good enough? Are you making an assumption that someone doesn't like you?" After your inquiry, you can go back to chapter 2 and do the end-of-chapter take-away exercise and process your emotions. Remember, your worthiness does not depend on anyone else! This doesn't take any value away from you. Keep your heart open and know that you are a beautiful soul with much to offer your new friends. Be a good friend to yourself—one who is unconditionally loving and kind.

Accepting Your Body

As we move into full acceptance of our bodies, we need to anchor ourselves in the belief and perception that aging naturally and gracefully is beautiful. A concept that changed my relationship with my body was an understanding that we *borrow* our bodies for this earthly life. We don't own our bodies. I have adopted the belief that the physical body belongs to Mother Earth. Our body is its own separate energy construct. From this perspective, I view my body as my friend, with respect and reverence. We work together like a partnership. I care for my body by managing my thoughts, processing my emotions, eating healthy foods, exercising, doing yoga, and tuning in to my body and responding to its needs. The body is a beautiful, intelligent configuration that does the best job it can for us. Your body is built to communicate perfectly with you. Each emotion is saying something. Each physical sensation is saying something. And we have a choice in how we respond: ignore it, hate it, accept and embrace it, listen and respond in a positive, loving, and proactive manner. Do you accept your body just as it is? If not, where is your resistance? Are you willing to accept and love your body? Your body is a beautiful physical representation of who you are and allows you to have the experience of being a human being on earth.

Unconditional Acceptance of Others: No More Blame

In full empowerment, we no longer place blame on another person or situation for causing us pain. Placing blame is imposing our own reality on someone else.

Let's say someone blames their parents for not showing enough love and positive support during their upbringing, and this person spends many years holding on to sadness and anger. Notice when you find yourself complaining over and over about a particular person. Blame is a way to eject our uncomfortable feelings toward someone else or something else, but the pain is still within us. To heal, we become responsible for our own feelings, perceptions, thoughts, and beliefs by recognizing that our well-being is a priority. We ask questions such as *what would happen if I decided to stop blaming that person? How long am I going to stay the victim in my story? Why am I choosing to hold on to this pain? Am I ready to be free?*

When we have the desire to be responsible in all ways, we draw our power back and stop blaming others. We are ready to be at peace. We all move through layers of awareness, in our own perfect timing for all our lessons. It can be scary to put a story aside, step into our sovereignty, and take responsibility for who we are as adults. Ignoring our pain and anger will not make them disappear. We may think that if we don't talk about them, the anger and hurt feelings will go away on their own, but they actually get stored in the subconscious and contribute to our overall vibrational level.

Complaining about someone or something is a waste of precious time and energy. It's the opposite of a vibration of unconditional love and full empowerment. It places us in the "victim" energy. Instead of listing the things you don't like about someone, one option is to say, "I accept you. I allow this situation. I accept that this is how you are choosing to behave." Move back into your infinite resourcefulness, infinite perceptions, and infinite options—back into your infinite power. At the same time, if it feels right for you, you can choose to move your energy in a different direction. But you can do it without judging the other person, without making them wrong or bad. You can choose not to dance with their particular vibration. There are many other frequencies. Choose the frequencies you want to dance with. Say, "I choose to plug into the highest frequencies of love, goodness, truth, and light. I intend to allow space for differences.

I invite the Divine's love into my heart. I choose to focus on solutions and opportunities."

During a workshop I gave on the topic of acceptance, two of the attendees shared stories of their challenges growing up, and the deficiencies in their parents. They both had scripts that were pointing blame toward their parents. Their emotional pain was holding them shackled to their story. To move beyond the pain and hurt in our own story, we have to be willing to accept who we are and accept our life exactly the way it is. We drop the story and take responsibility and personal accountability for our feelings and for who we are today.

One day, I tuned in to how I was feeling, and noticed I was carrying a little bit of anger around with me. It was very subtle but, nevertheless, still there. In contemplation, I allowed the anger to speak to me. I realized that this anger stemmed from blame that I had for someone. I was blaming them for my feelings. As a responsible adult, I knew I didn't want to be a victim, so it was necessary to let this go and move into full acceptance of both of us. This awareness was a blessing and a gift because it allowed me to take my power back and move deeper into love. If we catch any little subtle feeling of anger, this is a red flag that we may be blaming something outside us. And it's an opportunity to move into acceptance.

Unconditional Acceptance of Others: No More Judgment

I was seeking a healthier way to observe—a way to see without judging. I felt better inside when I took the time to get to know someone and found things I really liked. I made the decision not to speak in a derogatory way about anyone. In a meditation, I asked God a question. I said, "My intention is not to think or verbalize negative things about anyone. How can I like people more?" What I heard very clearly was this: "Everyone is doing the best they can. Focus on being and sharing light. Don't attach to how people show up or who they are." Keep your focus on your own intention and don't be concerned with what someone is or isn't doing or how they are acting. They are doing the best they can. For example, if you are taking a walk and you pass someone and say hello and they don't respond, practice not making that person wrong or bad. Practice keeping your energy contained and sending love. It's not our job even to guess why someone's behavior is the way it is.

If our energy zooms in on all the reasons someone is wrong, or acting poorly, this contributes to feelings of separation. We are judging, internally dictating how they should be and correcting them. We are telling ourselves, "I don't like her, because she is _____." [Fill in the blank.] When this happens, stop and notice what you are thinking. Tell yourself, "I will now stop condemning him. I choose to find something to like about her. I allow them to be." It doesn't mean you need to spend your personal time with this individual. You use your discernment to determine whose energy feels good to you, and navigate your energy in a direction that is aligned with the frequencies you prefer. It's a preference. You are discerning without judging. The other person's vibration is just not a match for you at this time. It doesn't mean they are bad or less than you. You understand that this person is a divine being, too, and that this is how they are choosing to express themselves at this moment.

Here's an example of how you can work on acceptance. Say you are driving in your car behind someone who's going ten miles an hour under the speed limit while you're trying to get to work. Instead of getting angry (maybe even cursing) or giving them dirty looks as you finally pass them, practice being an instrument of peace. Say, "I accept this moment. I am at peace in this moment. I don't sweat the small stuff." And put a big grin on your face.

It's easier to point the finger at someone else than to spend time owning our own energy. At times, we focus on what is wrong in others, or pass judgment on how they should be, as a distraction from looking at our own stuff. If you are making frequent judgments about others, spend some time looking to see what lies underneath this. If you are condemning them, take a moment to notice: Are you impatient? Do you feel like you are not in control? Are you afraid you are going to be late? Are you making them less than you in some way? If you answered yes to any of these questions, this is a good time to explore why you feel that way.

Each time I drove into a specific gated community, I stopped at the gate, said good morning, and gave my reason for being there. I then looked ahead for the gate to open so I could drive in. But when a particular guard was at the gate, inwardly I rolled my eyes because I felt he was too slow and his jokes were not funny and because I was, of course, in a hurry. I would say to myself, he's so slow, he's not funny, and he should be at the gate, paying attention. These thoughts were not respectful, not honoring this man's spirit. I saw my behavior loud and clear. In my mind, I silently said to this man's spirit, "I'm sorry, please forgive me." I offered respect for this man's soul, reminding myself that we are equals, and that he, just like all of us, is a blessed child of the Divine. I blessed this man and changed my perception to one of gratitude and appreciation toward him. The energy completely changed for me. I had love for this man whom I barely knew, and I was looking forward to seeing him again instead of feeling a twinge of disappointment when I saw him at the gate. A few days later, when I arrived at the gate with my newfound appreciation for this gate attendant, I gave him my full attention, with eye contact, and told him to have a great day. From then on, I had only respect for this man.

To connect with others, we acknowledge their divinity. We all are created from one source of unconditional love. There is no "better than" and no "worse than." The thoughts that we have for others matter. We are putting that energetic vibration into the universe and toward another person.

"When we seek to discover the best in others, we somehow bring out the best in ourselves."

—William Arthur Ward

For years, my brothers and I were unhappy with my dad's dietary habits, and we were always telling him what he should and shouldn't eat. And then one day, I was set free. My dad and I spent the day in the emergency room, and as we were leaving I was talking to the doctor about my dad's eating habits. The doctor said very matter-of-factly, "Your dad is turning eighty-four. Let him eat what he wants and enjoy himself." I said, "Okay," and from that moment on, I let go of the angst of trying to change his diet. I understood that he was getting immense enjoyment out of his food. I couldn't convince him to change his diet anyway. It would only have made him miserable. I stopped bucking the current and accepted his choices in full peace. It was actually a relief to let it go.

It can be challenging to watch our loved ones live in ways that we consider not the healthiest. We can offer our advice and encourage them, but at the same time accept and respect the choices they make in life, and the reality they create for themselves. Everyone has their own individual soul purpose, and we must allow them to express themselves in their own individual way and be who they are. This is unconditional love. Know that the energy of who you are has a positive effect on others around you. Your seeds of wisdom, love, and support get planted within the consciousness of your loved ones. Love is always effective, whether you see it or not!

During a workshop I was giving, a lovely woman shared with everyone her difficulties with her daughter-in-law. She expressed her frustration with all the things her daughter-in-law did wrong. At the same time, she told us her expectations of how a good daughter-in-law should behave. Family dynamics are very sensitive, and at times it can feel as though, no matter what comes out of our mouth, it seems to be the wrong thing. Anytime we blame something or someone we become a victim. If you find yourself in this position, ask, "What is the most fully empowered perception and belief I can choose?"

From experience, when I place expectations on how others should behave I am not fully embracing reality. I'm not fully accepting others with unconditional love. I'm being conditional. I'm judging and being critical. To raise my vibration, I ask, "How can I be accepting and loving? How can I let people just be who they are, with an understanding that they are who they are meant to be? Why allow others to affect my emotions and take me out of inner peace?"

We are responsible for our own energy, not for others. It's not our job to change people. The more we accept who we are, the less critical we are toward others. A workshop attendee of mine shared with the group how upset and frustrated she got, for years now, speaking to her sister on the phone. She listed all the reasons why. I asked her if she would be willing to let her sister be just as she was. Her sister had not changed in over forty years. Was it a good time to accept her for who she was without wishing she were different and without making her wrong? "Allow her to be *her*," I said. "She is not you. She operates with her own fears, her own insecurities, her own life experiences, her own perceptions, and a different life reality. But that doesn't mean it's a *wrong* way. She is doing the best she knows how. Can you love her for however she shows up? Can you open your heart and connect to her heart?" Loving someone doesn't mean just taking any old kind of disrespectful behavior from them. You can certainly limit your exposure to them and the time you spend in conversation with them. Loving someone doesn't mean you agree with their choices. But remember, *their* choices don't reflect who *you* are. Embracing and accepting reality keeps us in peace.

Moving from Anger and Hurt to Acceptance

Many of us have anger and hurt feelings that we are holding on to, both consciously and subconsciously. We all have had some kind of trauma or unhappy occasions and feel the pain of these life experiences. Take quiet time to be aware of your feelings, discern where the anger or hurt is coming from, and find the desire to let go of the pain and the strong connection to the story. Give yourself permission to stop suffering, stop beating yourself up, stop hating someone else, and stop making yourself bad. Let yourself come out of your inner prison. Forgive yourself for all the past choices and life situations that you don't feel proud of. You are now ready to be more compassionate and understanding. Moving into an attitude of choosing to *understand* looks like this: "I bless the person I was then, and I understand that I did the best job I could with the tools I had at the time. I accept and understand my past choices, and I forgive myself."

These experiences were lessons from your past. It's time to release the pain and set yourself free.

In many families, there is strife between siblings and between siblings and parents, and one person or both may have decided to disengage—to check out. This can cause stress within the family. If this is you, and you carry a deep, heavy sadness or anger in your heart, please consider taking quiet time to meditate and process your emotions, to bring yourself back into harmony. To raise your vibration, you move out of blaming and resenting the other person. It's not productive to fall into the role of martyr by heaping blame on yourself. To get into a space of inner peace, totally and completely accept the situation that is occurring, without wishing it were different and without wishing the other person were different. Trust that this is how life is meant to be *at this time*. If you feel guilty or you have anything to take responsibility for, then by all means communicate what is necessary to free up your heart. Get into a space of unconditional love for all parties; move into a higher vibration beyond right and wrong. We can disengage in peace and love and heal our hurt feelings. We can come together with new eyes of love and respect. Say, "I choose to change to the channel of love, seeing the love and goodness in everyone."

If you are ready to be free and move into acceptance, drop into your heart. Here's a quick and easy tool for getting into your heart: Imagine a ladder between your brain and your heart. You are in your mind at the top of the ladder. Get on the ladder and climb down the ladder, toward your heart. As you reach the last step you jump off and step directly into your heart. Rest in love. We begin to ask questions. These questions help trigger the answers within you. They help you discover the path to what you desire. Ask, *how can I move into my power? How can I begin a closer relationship to my wholeness? How do I release my sadness, hurt, and anger? How can I validate myself? How can I heal? How can I change my script?*

What do I need to believe in order to shift my way of thinking? Why am I holding on so tightly to my anger? Am I afraid to let it go? What would happen if I did? What would happen if I stopped making something wrong or bad? If you were to ask yourself these questions and *really* listen for the answers, you would be free and unshackled.

Unconditional Forgiveness

Forgiveness is for yourself. It is an act of self-love that will help you feel lighter, more joyful, and more empowered. Your emotions are not attached to a person or experience any longer. This doesn't mean you condone someone's behavior. It means you wish to set yourself free of your anger and hurt feelings toward the other person. It means you have a stronger desire to move back to inner peace and harmony. *Forgiveness changes your present and future.*

You will notice that when you change your beliefs that your emotions, too, will change. Try on these new beliefs: *I deserve to be happy. I believe I have a choice. I choose to have a new belief system that is more empowering, and I believe this is the road to inner peace. I believe that each person does the best they can and that everything is divinely orchestrated. I accept that everyone is different. Each individual has his or her own beliefs and values, just as I do. I am learning how to love myself, how to draw my power back to myself. I understand that the things in my life that make me really angry are showing me the areas that are*

Unconditional Acceptance and Forgiveness: No More Judgment

out of alignment within myself. I believe I can heal. I believe I have control over my behavior. I trust myself. I believe in myself. I accept my life. I understand how this situation is divinely perfect. This person didn't knock me out of a state of acceptance; this person merely triggered what was already in me. I am responsible for my emotions. I believe that this is an infinite universe. I trust this process. I accept this process.

Let's practice a more powerful script! Write this in your journal so you can read it daily. This script is now coming from a higher perspective, a place that knows you are now free and healed. Make a commitment to vocalize and believe your new script.

Here's an example of a new script: *"I accept the situation fully. I am choosing to heal! I let go of all my hurt, anger, and blame. I release my desire to punish the person who hurt me. I don't have to be right. I completely, unconditionally forgive them. I forgive myself. I choose to be 100 percent responsible for my words and behaviors. I intend to stay in alignment with my divinity. I understand that the behaviors of _____ [insert name] are not personal. Their behavior is aligned with their own fears, insecurities, and level of awareness. They did the best job they could. I accept _____ [insert name]. I fully honor _____ [insert name] as a divine being. I am sorry for my actions and words that may have caused pain. Please forgive me. I value myself! I learned a really good lesson. I send them love and happiness! I don't condone their actions, yet I unconditionally forgive them. I draw my energy back to myself. I move into a deeper level of love. I feel lighter and free!"*

At the end of this chapter, practice the "Unconditional Forgiveness" process and any other forgiveness exercise you are familiar with.

Once you're ready to release your pain and anger you can tap on your acupressure points with a meridian-tapping technique. As you tap you can say, "Even though I have this anger and hurt, I deeply and completely love and accept myself, releasing this anger, disconnecting this anger from my body, from my energy system and all functions in the body, letting go." Do a few rounds of releasing, and then tap on the specific meridian points while repeating higher-vibrational words such as "I am at peace; I am healing; I'm complete; I forgive; I am letting go, setting myself free; I am free; I feel good; I'm grateful."

Take-Away Exercises: Acceptance

Infinite Love and Acceptance Body Exercise

Sit or lie down in a comfortable place. Close your eyes. Relax. Take several deep breaths in through the nose and out through the mouth. Relax your mind. Say silently, "I connect with love from the Divine. I connect my energies with the highest realms of love and light. I breathe this infinite love into myself. I breathe love into my knees. I see my knees as strong, healthy, and happy." Place your awareness on your knees. Feel this love penetrating into the tissues in your knees—into the skin, the ligaments and tendons, the cartilage, the bones, into every cell. Say, "I breathe infinite love into my hips." Let your awareness sink into every tissue and cell of your hips. Imagine your hips as healthy, happy, and strong." Feel love around the hip area, trusting and knowing that divine love is there. Breathe in infinite love into your shoulders. Relax the shoulders. Imagine your shoulders as strong, supple, healthy, and happy. Breathe infinite love into your hands. Breathe. Bring your awareness to your hands. Feel the infinite love massaging through the skin and going deep into every cell of your hands. Continue doing this through your entire body and all its functions, including the musculoskeletal, cardiovascular, respiratory, digestive, immune, lymphatic, endocrine, reproductive, integumentary, excretory, and sensory and nervous systems. Say, "I am increasing the flow of life force into all my functions, into my cells, and increasing my mental capacity. All the cells in my body are my friends! My body loves me!"

Next, breathe infinite love into the base of your spine. Bring your awareness there. Feel love there. Bring your awareness to your lower belly. Breathe in infinite love into your lower belly. You can see infinite love as light of a platinum, gold, or white hue. Amplify this infinite light and love into a sphere extending four feet in front of you and four feet behind you. Move your awareness to the upper belly. Breathe infinite love into your upper belly. Place a hand there and feel the love there. Amplify this infinite light and love to fill the space extending four feet in front of you and four feet behind you. Move your hand to your heart. Breathe infinite love into your heart. Stay present here, breathing. Feel divine love inside your heart and at the back of your heart. Amplify this light to fill a bubble extending four feet in front of your heart and the same distance behind you. Move your hand to your throat. Say, "I breathe infinite love and light into my throat." Stay present here. Feel the love. Amplify this infinite light and love till it reaches out four feet in front of you and four feet behind you. Move your hand to your third eye, in between and just above your eyebrows. Say, "I breathe infinite love and light into my third eye." Stay present here. Feel the love. Amplify this infinite light and love until it extends to four feet in front of you and four feet behind you. Bring your hand to the top of your head. Say, "I breathe infinite love and light into the top of my head." Stay present here. Feel the love. Breathe. Now feel and see this infinite light and love in you and all around you grow to eight feet in diameter. Revel in this expansion of yourself. Marinate in this love. Set your intention to hold this image and feeling of love with you all day.

Unconditional Forgiveness Exercise

Write a letter to yourself forgiving yourself for every time you were not there for yourself, each time you gave your power away. Say, I'm so sorry for _____ [List a dozen—or a hundred or a thousand—things you are sorry for.]

Unconditional Forgiveness Visualization Technique

Begin with this prayer: "God, please help me release any uncomfortable feelings, anger, and frustration that I am carrying with me. I give every part of my being permission to release these emotions. Please help me have a wider view of life."

Close your eyes. Relax. Breathe in through your nose and out through your mouth. Bring the breath all the way down to your belly. On the in breath, expand your belly outward. Relax the mind. Breathe in unconditional love from the highest source of love. With this love, fill a sphere around you that is eight feet in diameter. Feel this love below your feet, above your head, and all around you. On your next breath, breathe in the highest frequencies of love and light into your entire body. With your eyes closed, imagine scanning your body for any pain, anger, and hurt that you are holding on to. Set your intention: "I am scanning my body for the pain, anger, and hurt that I'm holding on to." When you sense emotion place a hand over where you feel that the emotion is located. Breathe in through the nose and out through the mouth. Say out loud, "I'm ready to unconditionally forgive _____." [Insert the person's name.] Take a big breath, and on the exhalation, forcefully release your breath through your mouth and remove your hand. Imagine that you just let go and released the emotions. Say out loud, "I send all this energy back to the owner, _____!" [Insert the same person's name.]

Send the person love and light from the Divine. Breathe in love and light into your newly created spaces.

EVOLVING AND EXPANDING YOUR AWARENESS RAPIDLY

Let me begin by describing what it means to awaken and evolve. As you awaken you open up to an expanded awareness, taking on a larger view—a greater view, outside yourself, which makes you conscious of something bigger than what you knew before. Expanding our consciousness is a shift in perception and belief and personal insight. It's as if we had turned on a light switch allowing us to experience more life. This expansion is never-ending. Imagine your life right now as having a particular scope in the way you view things, possibly from beliefs you adopted from your environment as a child. This is the box that you are in. One day, you experience a shift in your perspective, which pushes the box's walls outward, making it a bigger box. And then, as life continues and you have more experiences, your mind opens up and you begin to change some of your old beliefs—perhaps becoming more accepting of others—which propels you into a still larger box. Eventually, you're outside all the boxes altogether. When you get outside all the boxes, there is no more us and them, no more blaming or feeling that we are better than others, no judgments that "they" are wrong, no anger toward others. There is no more big emotional charge that takes us out of a peaceful state. It's a space of full acceptance, peace, oneness, and understanding, of respecting each person as an equal and divine sovereign individual. It is a place of pure potentiality, where infinite creativity and possibilities live. When we live outside all the boxes there are no labels. It is a place of freedom, expansion, joy, and full empowerment. This is where we all are headed. We are waking up to our pure essence.

Evolving can be as subtle as noticing that you have the freedom to choose what feels best for you. We come to understand that our perspective and beliefs can be infinite.

A friend of mine ended her year-long relationship with a man and felt like a failure. I asked her if she would be open to hearing a different perspective, and she said yes. I told her, "I view your relationship as a divine experience. You both helped each other grow. You had some really nice experiences together, and now your time is meant to be over." We chatted about all the ways she grew and what she learned about herself in that relationship. That relationship also helped her define what is important to her. Now she understood that her energy was meant to go in a new direction. Just because a relationship ends does not mean it was a failure! Not all relationships are meant to be "till death do us part." A positive perspective is to trust that your relationship was a chosen experience for you at that time. She agreed and has since moved on to a whole new world of possibilities with new friends.

We often judge a breakup as a negative event because, during the heartbreak, we are sad and disappointed. We can be sad and disappointed and still have an understanding that we are meant to move on. Looking at it from this expanded view, the relationship was "an experience."

To shift our perception to a higher level is to say we *understand that there is a bigger picture and meaning for this past relationship*. With this perspective, we accept that it was meant to be. We trust life. We believe that we have the power to create our lives and choose beliefs that create the most powerful feeling within us. As we evolve we can catch ourselves when we are fearful, and bring ourselves back to a state of trust more quickly and easily.

Here's a helpful affirmation to use in moving from fear to trust:

Say, "I ask to feel my beautiful, luminous light essence. I expand into my light. Connected to unconditional love, I stand as this radiant light being drawing to me the highest frequencies of love and abundance and all my heart's desires. I draw to me the resources, the people, the support, and the opportunities to help me achieve my goals. I AM ETERNALLY GRATEFUL. Thank you!"

These scenarios below are examples of what it's like to evolve. Read through these life stories and see if you have had similar experiences.

- John routinely sat at the dinner table and ate without any regard for anything except filling his belly. One day, he saw a program on television about organic gardening. He started thinking differently about his food. He began thinking about the farms his food came from and the workers on the farm. He began to wonder, *were the farmers happy when they picked those vegetables?* He thought about the trucks that drove the vegetables across the country, and asked, *do the truck drivers enjoy their jobs?* John began wondering what kinds of pesticides were sprayed on the vegetables and whether they were harmful. With this expanded view, he evolved beyond his narrow focus of merely satisfying his hunger.
- One night as I lay in bed preparing to sleep, I caught myself reviewing my daily worries. I heard the message loud and clear: "No more worries. It's time to enjoy life *now*." This was a strong revelation. I didn't need to bring nightly worrying into my present and future! My whole body and mind relaxed. Give yourself permission to enjoy your life right now! Use your mind in a productive manner that demonstrates unconditional love and support.
- Jane had her initials on her car's vanity license plate. She got an inspired idea in her head that instead of

having a vanity plate that was all about her, why not change it to offer something positive and uplifting to all the people who drove behind her. This is a good example of thinking outside oneself.
- Stephanie was waiting for her boyfriend to pick her up and he was late. This was not a regular occurrence. Instead of getting angry with him for being late and taking it personally by focusing on her own inconvenience, Stephanie expanded her mind to consider what could be going on with him. She was thinking, *I wonder if he's stuck in traffic. That must be frustrating for him! I'm sure there is a good reason why he's not here yet."* She was thinking of him instead of herself.
- I noticed a pattern of mine. In a particular situation, I became aware that I was making a couple of particular people's work more important than my own. In this blessed state of awareness, I decided that I owed myself an apology. I needed to acknowledge that I was being conditional and was not validating my work. Silently I said, "I'm so sorry! Please forgive me. I love you." Your job, career, and what you offer here on earth are just as important as anyone else's. It is our culture that casts one career as more important than another. We are just as important as anyone else, and everyone else is just as important as we are, whatever our race, religion, or sexual orientation. My point here is this: please value what you offer. You are important. Say, "I'm important!" In the higher realm, there is infinite respect and reverence for each

other. Each spirit *knows* how important each radiant being is. We on earth are learning to walk back to this remembrance. When we do really *know*, we won't need to practice, read affirmations, or be reminded. We will just *be*.
- Sam noticed one day that he was not engaging in his same habit of thinking so negatively. He realized that he must have healed his past traumas and was no longer energetically dancing in that same vibration.
- A coaching client of mine, whom I will call Mike, booked a session with me. He was expressing his fears of how his family and wife would feel if he were to follow his heart and get separated from his wife. Mike had lived over forty years allowing his parents to control him. His fear and anxiety overwhelmed him to the point that he could barely speak and had trouble vocalizing his feelings. Through our sessions, he learned the importance of connecting to his authentic self and being real, which meant having the courage to say what he really felt. Over a couple of weeks, Mike had the courage to engage his wife in an open and honest dialogue, expressing everything that he had been feeling for roughly ten years. It was very challenging for both of them. He found his voice. He mattered. He had the courage to believe in himself.
- During meals, Jan grew up not accustomed to saying dinner prayers, but as she developed a greater awareness for life, she created her own ritual of giving

thanks to Mother Earth for the food she was eating, and blessing the spirit of each food item.
- On my morning walk, my dog Lexy came to a complete stop, anchored her body down, and pulled her neck back, yanking me backward. It was annoying! It was her way of directing me to what *she* wanted to do, which was her customary behavior. After a challenging night with her waking me up at 1:30 a.m., I had the epiphany that it was time for me to take more control over my life. My life was showing me this right then and there. I thought about how I could take this message into all areas of my life. I asked myself, *where in my life am I waiting and allowing something or someone to direct me?* I applied this message to my relationships with others and to my career.

Think of your life as a blank canvas. You can create whatever you like on your canvas. Are there areas in your life where you can take more control? Do you allow others to move you around? Do you sit by the sidelines and let life pull you around? How can you take more control of your life? What do you want to paint on your canvas?

As we evolve, some our friendships may change, too. If you have a relationship in which it is very challenging for you to be around that person, pay attention to how you feel. You may choose to create boundaries or move your energy in a new direction. A friend of mine shared with me that she had the awareness that every time she was around a particular person she didn't feel good; she felt drained. My friend chose to let a few months go by before seeing her friend. She explained that she felt bad for distancing herself. I told her, "I understand. At the same time, that is an act of self-love. Paying attention to how you feel and honoring yourself is self-care." As we continue evolving whatever is out of integrity will be illuminated for us to make the most authentic, highest choice. You are being asked to be very authentic in all ways, in all your relationships, especially your relationship with yourself.

Other evidence of evolving includes being able to:

- get into a state of peace more quickly than the normal pattern.
- choose unconditional acceptance and respect for others and self.
- use positive thoughts more than negative thought.
- spend more time focused in productive ways.
- open up to someone else's point of view without having to add your opinion.
- be patient more often than not.
- send positive thoughts and wishes to others.
- spend more time living in the moment with trust and love.
- be courageous and try something new that is aligned with your heart.
- walk away from a relationship with trust.

- observe another person's energy and choose not to jump into it.
- verbalize your feelings and boundaries for yourself.
- follow your heart and trust your intuition.
- live more of the time with a heart full of gratitude.
- accept faults in others and yourself.
- take responsibility for your energy instead of blaming others.
- forgive and let go more quickly and more easily.
- laugh at your silliness and feel your joy.
- allow others to shine in your presence.
- recognize the gift in your lessons.
- create healthier living habits.
- use your imagination and creativity to think outside the box.
- believe and value yourself.
- change from "What can I get?" to "How can I give?"

An Awakened Cleansing that Set Me Free

I had the realization that I had many more disappointments than major high points in my life. This awareness came about after an experience I had that triggered a whole avalanche of disappointment and sadness. In a meditation, I asked my higher self for guidance on the bigger message. I knew it was a waste of time and energy to be angry with the person who triggered this latest experience. I went into the emotion of this sadness.

There are layers to healing, and I knew that this was a deeper layer I was processing. I also had the awareness pop in that said, "What if this was a huge cleansing of many years of disappointment and sadness so that the rest of your life can be different? You will live with many more high points. How would that feel?" I took a deep breath, and I could hear a gurgling sound in my belly, like a big release.

I did a couple of rounds of meridian tapping on the disappointment and sadness and I processed the emotions. I have an understanding that my disappointments throughout my life taught me that I need to recognize myself and truly see *me*. What if this is the case for you, too? What if now is the time to recognize lower-vibrating emotions within you, to assist you on your path into wholeness, into your full sovereignty?

My Divine Shift of Personal Power in the Romance Arena

I received a lengthy e-mail from a person whom I will call Liz. I had met her over a decade ago and hadn't seen her since. At the bottom of the e-mail she asked me if I wanted to meet a friend of hers. She felt that he and I would have a lot in common. When I replied to her, I brushed aside her invitation to meet her friend. In the next e-mail from her, she mentioned him again. So I took the time to explore the person. I replied that yes, I would love to meet her friend. She gave him my contact information and said he was going to call me. A week went by and I didn't hear from him; then another week went by, another week, and another. Each time

I saw Liz I mentioned it to her. She texted him and he said he was busy and he was going to contact me. A couple of months went by, and no phone call. In the meantime, I was still holding tightly to the thought of meeting him. He was still saying he wanted to meet me, but he never got around to it. I was attached to meeting him, until I finally had a huge shift. This shift set me free! In a meditation, I received intuitive information: "Let it go. Pull your energy back. Value yourself and believe you deserve someone who will respond."

This was a shift into my wholeness. My intention during this time was focused on feeling my wholeness, experiencing my sovereignty. This experience was a divine gift. I believe it was divinely orchestrated for me to have this growth experience. It can be such a surprise how things work out! I knew that I needed this to fully value myself so that I never have to repeat old patterns again. This is freedom. I don't have the "neediness" feeling or the vibration that I lack anything anymore. It's powerful! I feel complete. I feel comfortable. It feels like freedom! It feels powerful. It feels like love.

How do I know that I shifted? By observing how I felt. One day, as I was out taking a walk, I felt this feeling of oneness with the beautiful nature all around me—oneness with the lake, the sky, the ducks and other birds. I was not feeling lonely or wishing a man was next to me experiencing this moment. Another observation: I didn't have any interest in this particular man calling me anymore. I had the realization that I deserved a match to my energy. I felt more love and inner peace. I moved out of a *need*, to a *want*. And that is something very different.

This is what it's like to step into our wholeness without suffering. As we continue to awaken, this is what is offered to all of us as we continue to step away from the victim role and into the fully empowered being role. It's exhilarating! We are expanding into more of our own light, becoming brighter light beings. Call on the light within. Say, "I choose to explore my light from within. I choose to amplify my light, to feel it and know that it exists."

Continuing on Your Evolving Path: No More Suffering

You are capable of activating your divinity. Choose your own reality—not one that is put on you, or one that you think you should live in. Choose a reality based on knowing that your energy is infinite, expansive, and vast. From this mentality, what are your desires? Keep your focus on those desires. Do you believe that you live in a world of infinite possibilities?

We shed the layers of our conditioning and continue moving forward, to our authentic self. It takes a lot of inner strength, trust, and courage to stay on this path. On this path, you may feel alone at times, but the rewards are like none you have ever experienced. You have come home to yourself.

I have watched many videos of spiritual teachers speaking on many different aspects of life. I discerned a resonance with the teachers who didn't have a personal agenda of being perceived in a particular way. This was a lesson for me to continue just being me, with no agenda for how I want to be perceived, with no energy of control on how I should be "seen."

This is freedom because when you truly get that, then you are free just to show up in life as your authentic self with no agenda.

This is exactly where the earth is headed: removing the walls and expanding our possibilities into the infinite. We also consider how we affect the whole, how we are connected, and how we can help the whole and live in harmony so it is mutually beneficial for all. Continuing on our path of awakening, we begin to think about the energy we are putting into the universe, the energy we add daily, and the footprint we are leaving behind.

As we each process our fears, increase our self-love, and trust in ourselves we all walk toward owning our wholeness. Therefore, we expand our awareness and ascend to a higher vibration without the need for pain and suffering. Suffering is from the duality of dark and light and spending too much time disconnected from our powerful infiniteness. As divine beings, we are waking up to unconditional love.

We have moved beyond reflecting back the shadow side of each other and learning through painful experiences. We are becoming awakened beings, grounded in the knowing of who we are, why we are here, and what we are meant to be doing. We are healing our wounds and disappointments and living in a higher vibration of love and light. The more we evolve, the more we and others reflect back to one other the truth of who we are: our loving, beautiful, joyful, intelligent, powerful side.

We are awakening to the concept of oneness. In Lynne McTaggart's book *The Field: The Quest for the Secret Force,*

McTaggart writes about astronaut Ed Mitchell's experience on the *Apollo 14* journey to the moon.

"Ed said that while looking out the window, 'there seemed to be an enormous force field here, connecting all people, their intentions and thoughts, and every animate and inanimate form of matter for all time.' Anything he did or thought would influence the rest of the cosmos, and every occurrence in the cosmos would have a similar effect on him." We are energetically connected to everyone. This is why we care so much about others.

As we are evolving we care more about people globally, not just in our own community or country. We care more about equity of resources for the people who are in need of clean water and proper nutrition to survive. We care more about our own health. We are waking up to healthier ways of eating. New evidence abounds regarding the benefits of eating healthful foods that contribute to living more vibrant, longer, more vigorous lives. This is all evidence that the human species is evolving into a more awakened, more empowered way to live. Can you imagine what life on earth will be like two hundred years from now? Look at how much living on our earth has changed since 1812! We are setting the stage for the future.

Jane's Big Change in Awareness

Jane said, "My mom verbally abused me. She told me I'm stupid and said I would never amount to anything. And called me ugly." Jane asked me, "How do I get beyond the pain? How do I feel better about myself?"

I replied, "If you were emotionally abusing your own child because of your own pain, how would you want your child to perceive the situation? I'm going to assume that you would want her to feel good about herself despite all the horrible treatment. Correct? You would want her to understand that you were responding from your own pain, because of your own lack of self-love, because you yourself were mistreated as a child. Perhaps you have not been exposed to a more loving way yourself. This does not excuse your Mom's behavior in any way."

I went on to say, "Despite all the harshness you poured out onto your child, you would want her to allow it to bounce off. You would want her not to personalize it and believe it. You would want her to feel good about herself as a strong, wise, beautiful, smart, and confident person." Jane agreed.

I said, "Let's focus on *you*. Let's begin with changing your perception and beliefs and create a new script—maybe something like this:

"My mom did the best she knew how at the time, with the tools she had. I'm an adult now, and as an adult, I am responsible for loving myself, and I do! I love myself for how far I've come, for how much I care about others, for my ability to show compassion, for my inner strength, for my wisdom, for my ability to love who I am today! The opportunity to learn about forgiveness has been a gift. I have learned to love that scared child within me."

Jane had a big release and began supporting her dreams and desires by truly awakening to her own heart. She saw her Mom with new eyes. She saw *herself* with new eyes. Jane evolved to another level of self-love and acceptance.

Take-Away Exercises: Expanding Your Awareness

Recognizing Your Own Growth

Please fill in the blank lines with your answers:

1. How have you grown personally in the past several years?
   _____
   _____
   _____
   _____

2. How have you demonstrated living life more lightly?
   _____
   _____
   _____
   _____

3. How have you grown in courage?
   _____
   _____
   _____
   _____

4. How have you demonstrated trust and love of yourself?

_____
_____
_____
_____

5. How have you expanded your awareness?

_____
_____
_____
_____

Prayer: Ask your guardian angels and the Divine to help you evolve in particular areas where you feel separate from your light. Ask to feel unconditional love and to know what it feels like to be a beautiful light being. Ask for help in feeling your sovereignty. See your inner strength glowing with radiant white light connected to the Divine.

5

EFFECTIVE COMMUNICATION SKILLS

We are always communicating. We communicate in many ways, not only by our oral and written words but also by the clothes we wear, the cars we drive and the way we drive them, how we carry ourselves with our actions and behaviors, the speed with which we move, the tone and pitch of our voice, the friendliness (or unfriendliness) of our attitude, our facial expressions—even the way we wear our makeup and hair. And let's not forget about the volumes of communication given out by our busy inner thoughts and feelings. The interior of our living space communicates that we are minimalists; clutter bugs; neat freaks; lovers of nature, art, or antiques. All our home decor, right down to the books in our bookcases and the tchotchkes on our knickknack shelves, tells a story. It all communicates something about us. Even our chosen profession and hobbies and romantic partners share a message about us. We are always expressing who we are. As we continue to evolve into more of our beautiful, divine nature, we reflect more of the essence of ourselves through all our communications.

The more we evolve into ourselves, we are leaving behind a combative communication style and replacing it with a more harmonious and peaceful connection. Aren't you eager for a higher level of communication, verbal integrity, and intimacy with others? Collaborating is much more fulfilling than competing can ever be. It's time to focus on finding common ground and seeking solutions that fit the needs of *everyone*. It's time to allow our true self to be seen. This respectful attitude toward others is a direct reflection of the love and respect we have for ourselves. In this time period, our language is from the heart—it's the language of unconditional love.

We have awakened into being more compassionate beings, and we *care* about the imprint we leave on others and on the earth. Passing on love and kindness creates a ripple effect of positive energy. Russian biophysicist and molecular biologist Pjotr Garjajev has found that a portion of our DNA serves as data storage in communication and that the human body is programmable by language. Our DNA and genes react to language, emotions, and thoughts. Words can actually alter a person's DNA. It's apparent that our hearts are calling out for a kinder reality—a more respectful, authentic, empowering, loving, and healthy reality. It begins with us being that way toward ourselves. You can alter your DNA by using unconditionally loving language.

Let's ponder this question for a moment: *what is a conflict?* A conflict is beliefs, ideas, or opinions being expressed *in an antagonistic state.* Why can't differences of opinion coexist in peace? We are always going to have differences of opinion with others. But it is vitally important to be able to let others have their opinions and for us to be okay with differences. Others do not have to agree with us. Just be open and listen. Can we listen to others with an open ear? Can we accept other people's opinions without trying to convince them that our way is the right way? Do we have to put our opinion on top of theirs? Listening with an open mind gives us opportunities to learn new things and connect more deeply with others. You do not have to agree with what the person is sharing. You can simply offer the energy of *"Yes, what you are sharing matters."* You don't have to prove them wrong. You can accept their view without having to disagree or agree. With this compassionate energy, during conflict or a challenge, you have far better odds of getting to the heart of the matter.

Not everyone will connect with us, and guess what: that is okay! Focus on all the people you *do* connect with. And don't take it personally like *something is wrong with you* when you are not connecting with someone. This reminds me of a fable from Aesop, shared by Joel Osteen. The story goes something like this: An old man and his son were walking with a donkey to the market when the old man heard a countryman say, "You fools, what is a donkey for but to ride upon?" So the man put the boy on the donkey, and they went on their way. But soon they passed a group of men who said, "Look at that poor old man walking while the young, fit boy gets to ride on the donkey!" So the man took the boy off the donkey, and *he* got on the donkey. They hadn't gone far when he heard

Language of the Heart: Unconditional Love

someone say, "Look at the poor little boy walking while the grown man gets to ride the donkey!" Well, the man didn't know what to do, but at last he picked up the boy and put him on the donkey in front of him. By this time they had come to the town, and the passersby began to jeer and point at them. The man stopped the donkey and asked what they were scoffing at. The men said, "Aren't you ashamed of yourself for overloading that poor donkey of yours with both you and the boy?" I loved this story. There's always going to be someone out there who doesn't like what we are doing or saying, but it's up to us to stay centered and at peace with our choices with no attachment to whether a person agrees.

The intention behind our words is important. It's our intention that is felt. If the intent of our message is to create a heart connection or to be helpful, the sincerity of our energy will be felt. If our intent is to hurt someone's feelings, embarrass them, or "teach 'em a lesson," we are not going to connect on a heart level. And the other person will likely feel the anger, selfishness, and judgment. We may not even be aware of our own intent, because our emotions are in the way or because we just didn't think about it. Before taking action, take a moment and ask, "What is my intention?" "How can I connect to my heart?" "What type of energy do I want to be in this moment?" "What end goal am I trying to achieve that is mutually beneficial to all?"

In a prayer, I asked for clarity about a particular situation. I was shown how the energy of my communication caused an adverse outcome in a business situation. I was in a short two-minute discussion with a couple of people. My intention was not in my heart. I was focused on getting something accomplished, instead of connecting. Over the phone, I did not come across as warm, inviting, or welcoming. I was narrowly focused on the logistics of making something happen. Unfortunately, the people I was talking to didn't know me, and it was not easy for them to *want* to get to know me at that point. I got a phone call the next day informing me they did not want to pursue the business situation with me. I did apologize several times and took complete ownership, and I tried to make it up to them. But the two minutes' damage had been done.

The interesting part of the story comes next. A few days later, I received a phone call, and I felt the same way the two women had felt with my communication. The woman was not in her heart. In both these situations, the goal was not achieved. It became vividly clear to me just how important it is to take a moment and be in our hearts before acting, before speaking, before making that phone call. And to take a moment and remind ourselves that here is this beautiful human being I am about to connect with, who deserves my complete respect. Once someone feels this connection, they are more apt to respond to us in a positive way.

As we continue to evolve, our ego becomes healthier, more balanced, and better integrated into our sacred self. This is what is happening now to all of us as we move along this evolved path. It's natural and life sustaining to desire a heart connection.

What does a heart connection look like? *Feel* like? A heart connection is looking into the eyes of another and sharing in the moment of joy and happiness; sharing in tears and sad emotions; sharing in common struggles; feeling understood, accepted, and supported; and feeling love flowing between two people or in a group of people. It's a shared moment of triumph and happiness for another person's success. It's a shared experience of working and creating together and finding solutions to another person's needs or problem. It's a moment of understanding someone else and expressing compassion, support, gratitude, or encouragement. One special heart connection moment that stands out for me is the time a yoga student walked up to me after class. She spoke only rudimentary English. She handed me a small token gift, held my hand in hers, placed her other hand on her heart, looked into my eyes, and nodded her head in thanks. We held this gaze for a few seconds as I felt her sincere love and gratitude. This gratitude I felt from her was palpable. It touched me on a deep level. You have had these moments throughout your life, too. These are the moments we remember. These are the moments that weave together the meaningful and fulfilling, beautiful tapestry of our lives. These are moments from our heart. The good news is, these moments gradually will become the greater share of our life moments.

> *"Occasionally in life there are those moments of unutterable fulfillment which cannot be completely explained by those symbols called words. Their meanings can only be articulated by the inaudible language of the heart."*
>
> —Martin Luther King Jr.

Being Present as a Listener

There are several aspects to being a good communicator as a fully empowered being. In this world of ever more sophisticated technology, many of us are connected to our iPhones, iPads, Blackberries, computers, and keyboards and busy with social media and texting throughout our day. It's inevitable that while multi-tasking we may miss half of a message shared by a friend, family member, boyfriend, girlfriend, or business associate. If we are not 100 percent engaged, we might guess at what we think may be the appropriate response. This is a missed opportunity to connect and show that you care. To fully engage with someone who is speaking, listen in a focused, attentive manner.

Listening with an attentive focus, full presence, and an open heart allows us to engage not just our ears but *all* our senses—and, in particular, our intuition. Others feel our loving intent. Practice listening fully, and this will increase your intuitive abilities. Bringing all your focused energy to the table is like bringing your gift of light and love to the table. If you are engaging in face-to-face communication, give the speaker plenty of eye contact. This allows the other person to feel energetically connected and *valued*. They will know that your intention is to hear and understand their communication *fully*.

As the listener, we allow the speaker to finish his or her own sentences and thoughts. Since our intention is to connect and listen, our body language reflects this by our calm, patient, friendly demeanor. When the speaker is finished, we keep the energy around their story sacred by making a comment or response directly related to what they shared. Before bringing the conversation back to yourself or imposing your agenda, revel in their energy for a moment. For example, say a person is really enthusiastic in sharing a story of something that happened to them, or something they learned. If they are exuding a vibration of joy, allow that joyful vibration to stay present before switching the energy to another topic—especially if that other topic is *you*. To keep the wonderful vibration going, join and support their blissful energy. Perhaps express what you appreciated or connected with in their message, or ask them a question about it. For example, you might say, "How did you feel?" "What did you enjoy the most?" "What did you find worked the best?"

Since 1985, Ernesto Sirolli did economic development training for leaders in three hundred communities on four continents. In a talk by Sirolli, he shared that one of his biggest mistakes had been his lack of listening—listening to the needs and the passions of others. He spoke about his mistakes when going to South Africa to teach them about his way of growing vegetables, only to find that it wasn't suitable for their terrain. He learned the importance of listening before imposing his agenda. In his training program, he teaches listening with the whole body.

If you are too busy to give your full attention, just be clear. Tell the person that you are busy right now and that you would prefer to give them your full attention. Offer another time or, if it's urgent, stop multi-tasking and LISTEN.

Our Options as a Listener During a Conflict

Listening with "Observation Ears"
You always have a choice while listening. If we can stay emotionally neutral and objective, we are able to listen as a witness and stay balanced and grounded in peace. In this space, we are open and accepting of the information. We are not passing judgment by making the information "wrong" or "bad." In this state, we observe and understand that life is not black and white. We recognize that others have their own personal experiences and beliefs, which may be different from our own. We understand that our own point of view may be healthy for us but not necessarily good for everyone. We have respect for other people's choices, beliefs, and opinions. The key here is *respect*. With respect as our intention while listening, the other person can feel our reverence. Even if we don't agree with what someone is saying or the choice they have made, we can still allow space for their point of view. This may be an opportunity to learn something new and expand our own awareness.

Being emotionally neutral is not allowing the comments or behaviors of others to take anything away from us. It's not a personal attack, and we don't feel threatened. We don't allow their energy to pull us into their "story." We understand that it's the other person's life experiences that are creating their feelings, perceptions, and beliefs. In this position, we offer our authenticity and our kindness. We are listening for information with a compassionate ear. In this state, we can listen with an open heart for the speaker's feelings and needs being expressed. We don't engage in the other person's emotions. We are calm, grounded, and peaceful. This is the most empowered state to be in.

Here is an inner dialogue of an objective listener: *I'm interested in understanding this person's intention and needs. I welcome this person here. I am going to be 100 percent present. I know that this person's behavior doesn't take anything away from me. I'm not going to personalize. I'm really going to listen in a neutral space, grounded in my own sovereignty. This person is making choices and expressing in a way that is directly aligned with his or her life experiences and beliefs, which is perfect for this person. I am open to another person having different beliefs from mine. I accept them. I'm an empowered being. I know that I have a choice, and I can listen with my heart and allow them to be in my presence. I'm going to let any negative comments bounce off me.*

Listening with Personalizing and Judgmental Ears

If we personalize what someone is saying, we have a belief that the other person's behavior or comment is devaluing us in some way. We hear a criticism, and we make the information about *us*. We may feel personally offended, disrespected, unloved, sad, or unworthy. In that moment, we give our power away and become a victim. We are emotionally buying into what this person said or did. We may even try to prove that we are right and they are wrong. This is not the most empowered state.

A person who is personalizing is thinking, *How dare they do that to me! I feel unloved,* or *I'm a failure,* or *I'm not a good person,* or *I'm not as talented, successful, or smart as they are,* or *they're mean and don't like me, and I feel misunderstood.* A person in this state is hurt. They may retaliate, criticizing the other person or defending themselves with comments (whether internal or spoken) such as *They are so stupid! They have no idea what they're talking about. What an idiot! I know so much more than they do. They are speaking so slowly, I wish they would get to the point. They are not that evolved and really should spend time changing their behaviors.* With judgmental ears, our thoughts and responses are apt not to be loving and kind.

If we become defensive, then the speaker does not feel validated or heard, and we are not likely to connect on a heart level. If you find yourself blaming the other person, catch yourself and see what needs to be healed within you. If we have an unresolved issue within ourselves, that particular issue within us, until healed, will be sensitive to us. Therefore, if another person triggers that area within us, we may likely respond from sadness or hurt. We temporarily forget that we are whole, that we are radiant light and are infinite, divine, powerful beings.

In our daily life, many of us bounce around—in one moment, we are listening as an observer, from an emotionally neutral place, and the next moment, we are judging and personalizing. Begin to be the witness to your own energy as you are listening.

If You Are the One Speaking

In many cases, if there is time before speaking to a person in a fraught situation, I meditate on the conflict first. I like to discern my part in the energy exchange, and the higher meaning. In many cases, I can process the situation, tune in to my intuition, discern my lesson, and receive guidance without even the need to speak to someone. There are times when I intuitively sense that verbal communication would not be necessary (or, perhaps, fruitful). And in many cases, during visualizations, I imagine standing in front of another person and sending them the energy of completely respecting their divinity, knowing that behind whatever behavior they are displaying, they are a unique, infinite, beautiful being. Many times during a conflict, the other person doesn't feel respected in some way. I will find one or two things that I admire about them, and place my focus on uplifting and celebrating those qualities in them. This way, my mind isn't focused on all the things I don't like about the person—which would only increase that energy of not feeling respected.

In conflicts with certain friends or associates, you may sense that it's not the right time for communication, or that the other person isn't open to hearing what you have to say. Or there may be a clashing of realities. If this is the case, it may be best to move your energy away, temporarily and with love. This is not about you feeling that you are right and they are wrong. This is looking at it from a higher perspective—one that respects both people's personal story and life journey. And if one person is holding on to their personal story so tightly that they can't open up to someone else's point of view, the healthiest action to take is to separate, peacefully and without blame. You have an understanding that all is in divine order and that this is exactly the way life is meant to be at this time. Set your intention: "I intend to accept this situation with peace and love. I choose to feel peace in my heart about this situation. I choose to let my inner light fill my heart with infinite love." You can send them good wishes and hold positive regard for them.

If you feel you are angry, disappointed, or upset, take time to process your emotions before you communicate. If you feel devalued in any way, look within yourself and give yourself the love and respect you deserve as a divine being of God. If you are personalizing the situation, look within and examine your own sensitivity and any expectations you may be harboring on how others should behave. If you feel that the behavior or energy from the other person was disrespectful, ask yourself, "Do I feel that I was conditional with myself during the interaction? Did I handle myself in a manner that was respectful to both parties? If not, why not?" Are you mad at yourself for not speaking up? Are you mad at yourself for exhibiting rage?

Allow your emotions to speak to you, accept them and welcome them. Stay objective. Remember, no judgment. Make a conscious decision to let all animosity go. And walk forward in trust that all is well. Keep processing your emotions daily until you can think of the other person with a smile on your face and in your heart at the same time. This can take days or even months, depending on the nature of the relationship.

This will allow time for you to gain a higher perspective and, possibly, to see how this experience gave you an opportunity to grow within yourself. As we continue to heal and awaken, we won't have as many conflicts with others. When we are triggered with strong emotions about something, it's our ego that is being triggered. The other person is the *facilitator,* not the cause. If you are blaming the other person, catch yourself and see what needs to be healed within yourself.

The way we react to life is showing us exactly what is going on inside us. As we all continue to ground within our light we respond to life in a loving and peaceful energy, using higher-vibrational language.

The next scenario is an example of communicating with respect, from a neutral place. I was teaching a beach yoga class for a resort chain. As I was walking the class onto the grassy area to our designated yoga spot overlooking the ocean, two men and two boys were having a football toss. We proceeded to walk down the other end of the grass section and lay the yoga mats down. The men continued their football toss, throwing the ball right toward us, and just missing us on a couple of occasions. They were clearly annoyed that we were there. About halfway through the class, the football almost hit one of my students in the head. I looked up, told my students to hold a yoga pose, and started walking toward the man who had thrown the ball. In a loud voice, he shouted, "We were here first!" I continued walking calmly. He yelled to me, "We're leaving in ten minutes." I kept on walking right up to him, looked at him in the eyes, and said calmly, "This is a regularly scheduled spa yoga class." He nodded his head, and they left immediately.

At the end of the yoga class, my students looked at me and said, "Wow, what did you say to him? They stopped their toss and said, 'Sorry' as they walked by us." It was simple: I didn't make them wrong or bad. I didn't engage in an argument. I just stated a fact in a calm tone of voice. I have certainly made many mistakes communicating in my past. As I grew in awareness, so did my communication style.

Your expression of your voice is powerful. The sound and tone of your voice says something about you. With your voice, you inform others and the universe how you feel and who you are. With your authentic voice, your innate power comes through.

Here is an example of a beautiful and successful heart-to-heart conversation during a conflict. Christina, a client of mine, arrived at our coaching session in tears. She was confused and worried by a sudden decision her husband had made to exclude her from being actively involved in what he considered "his" projects. His abrupt change in behavior triggered a mixed reaction in Christina. She was angry and hurt and caught up in her own wound of feeling unworthy. Her story was, "He doesn't value my opinion, so what value do I have in this marriage?" As we sat face-to-face, I listened to her explain her story. I was actually tuning in to how this experience "triggered" Christina. During our session, I asked her questions such as "What are you afraid of?" I repeated details in her story and asked her, "When he said that, how did that make you feel? Have you ever felt this way before?" I shared with her my intuitive empathic impressions of what I was sensing. This helped her clarify and define how she felt. I was slowly drawing her awareness and power back to herself. Each time she confirmed her feelings, I had her write each one down on a piece of paper. Up until this point, she hadn't expressed her feelings to her husband in a responsible way. Caught up in the fear of being rejected, she projected her anger onto him. I asked her, "Did your husband express his feelings using actual feeling words?" Christina said no, he gave his reasons but not his feelings.

Christina agreed to stop blaming her husband and take responsibility for her feelings. She and I discussed how our life stories trigger what is inside us. She astutely and earnestly admitted that these were her own self-love issues.

I suggested that she and her husband sit down and look into each other's eyes and have a heart-to-heart conversation. I told Christina that during this conversation, she should express her feelings and needs and give her husband the opportunity to express *his* feelings and needs. I went on to say, "Let each person finish speaking without the other person interrupting, making faces, or shaking their head. Maintain respectful body language."

She went straight home and, in a calm manner, asked her husband if he was willing to sit down and talk. With his agreement, Christina took out her piece of paper with her all her feelings jotted down. With an open heart, allowing herself to be vulnerable, she shared each *feeling* of hers along with her *beliefs*. She even admitted that her hurt reaction came from her own lack of self-love.

Christina's husband listened to her and expressed sympathy. He even told her he was sorry and that he did want her involved in the projects. He explained why he had made his abrupt decision, and confessed his feelings. She felt relieved and acknowledged.

Christina called me on the phone the next day and said, "I feel he understood me. I feel validated. All the tension between us just melted away." She went on to say that she had let go of all her worries and felt very comfortable. Christina took the time to process her perspective, her emotions, and figure out her feelings and get direction on how to communicate. She said, "It was tremendously helpful to have a clear focus in my conversation and not get sidetracked by laying the blame on him and getting too emotional. Expressing my *feelings* allowed my husband to relax and listen."

I'm proud of both of them. Both partners shared their feelings and needs, listened, expressed compassion, felt heard, and came to a happy resolution. I spoke to Christina a couple of months after this incident, and she told me they are doing great and she is helping her friends use this communication technique in their relationships.

In this next story, a client of mine had a couple of relatives who were perpetually late when meeting my client socially. This went on regularly for several years. My client expressed his frustration and anger to me. I asked him if he thought this was an opportunity for him to value and respect himself. I told him that one way to do that would be to get out of the web with these two relatives. My client agreed that his time was valuable and that this wasn't acceptable. He decided he was going to express his boundaries by stating a particular time that was his threshold; if they hadn't shown up by then, he would leave. I was really proud of him. His ability to express what would and what wouldn't work for him was successful with one of his relatives. This allowed my client to flex his personal empowerment muscle and declare what was acceptable to him. He was able to do so and still maintain a good relationship with one of his relatives. He felt really good about himself. This alleviated his frustration and anger and enabled him to enjoy the time he spent with that relative. Radical responsibility is a big part of self-growth and maturity. It's easy to ignore things and not deal with life. It takes courage to deal!

There are times when, for our own personal empowerment, it is necessary to speak up, especially if we are receiving unkind treatment. You are the one who determines what is best for you. Trust your inner guidance, trust how you feel, and use your voice at the appropriate time. A great question to ask yourself is, "What action feels the most loving and empowering?"

Successful Speaking Tips:

- Before speaking, set your intention to yourself. For example: "My intention for this communication is to express from my heart in the highest way possible, share my feelings, and connect with the other person in a respectful manner. I intend to have a truthful, loving, heart connection. I choose to respond calmly from a place of power. I intend to speak in a way that recognizes this person is an infinite divine being."

- If possible, confirm that you have the other party's full attention and that they are available to receive your communication.
- Maintain good eye contact with the listener.
- Use facts only. Be specific about the situation, time, date, and actions. Eliminate the need to embellish and exaggerate.
- Avoid words or phrases that will put someone on the defensive, such as "you always," "you never," "you should," "you are wrong," "what you need to do is," "everyone else thinks this, too." Don't tell the other person how they are feeling. Stay away from name calling, insults, bullying, pointing out negative things about the person, yelling, cursing, and running out of the room. Stay away from manipulation and control tactics.
- Express how you feel, using feeling words such as "lonely," "hurt," "scared," "uneasy," "worried," "angry," "surprised," "uneasy," "confused," "sad," "insecure," "dejected," or "discouraged." It's important to express your feelings on how a particular situation made you feel. Stick to using only feeling words, not descriptive words (such as "mean," "inconsiderate," "thoughtless," "arrogant," "unfair," and so on). Begin with "I feel," not "you made me feel," because the latter puts you in a victim mode—not an empowering energy. No one can make you feel a particular way unless you choose to feel that way.
- Express what you need in the form of a request. Keep your tone calm.

- Before making assumptions, ask questions to gather more information.
- Be honest. This is the most powerful energy there is.

Vocabulary of an Expanded Consciousness

As fully empowered beings, we care about the vibration of our language. Our language makes an imprint in our energy field, in the energy field of the person we are communicating with, and in the unified field of consciousness. It feels better to practice more inspiring, encouraging, loving, supportive, and positive self-talk. This new language is aligned with trust and love, with knowing that you are a loving, magical, infinite, fully empowered being. I still practice switching from worrying to asking myself, "What is the best-case scenario?" "What is going right?" "What do I like?" "How is the universe supporting me?" "How does this make me feel?" "What do I want?" "If I felt my wholeness, how would I feel?" "What is the most loving thing I can say to myself right now?" "What would I say to my best friend?" And then I spend time imagining my desires, with an action plan. Positive thoughts are thoughts that believe in successful results. Pay attention to your inner voice. Your inner voice is the voice of your soul. This is your personal language.

Language that Is Encouraging, Supporting, and Inspiring
Inspiring, joyful, and encouraging communication is the language of your heart. This language recognizes that you are an infinite, divine being. Here are some examples of

the language of your heart: You can practice reading these out loud—when you are by yourself, or others will wonder who you are talking to.

"I believe in you. I value your dreams. I know that you are a powerful person. You are so good at being resourceful. I trust that you will find a solution—after all, you always do. You did an amazing job. I really like you. You have such a beautiful heart. I love your courage to try new things. You did the best job you could, and you learned a very valuable lesson that will help you in the future. You are so good at being you! I'm tremendously proud of your tenacity and spirit for life. I'm so proud of your indomitable courage, immeasurable inner strength, lively spirit, and curiosity for life. You are beautiful, and I love you. I'm so impressed with what you accomplished. You have great people skills. I know you are going to do a great job. They are going to love you! You are going to learn a lot. Just have fun! You are a blessing. It's awesome that you are courageous enough to put yourself out there and be open to a new experience. I know you can do this. It's going to be a wonderful experience."

At the beginning of a yoga class, I asked my students to set their intention to have only positive thoughts toward themselves, for one full hour. After we did a balancing pose, I said to my students, "Raise your hand if you just said to yourself, 'I'm terrible at balancing.'" Sure enough, a couple of people raised their hands. But would we ever turn to our best friend and say, "You are terrible at balancing"? Is this supportive, encouraging, and loving? How about an inner dialogue that whispers, "I'm balanced and grounded"? And "I appreciate that I'm trying." Many times while I'm teaching yoga, when I've fallen out of a pose and I giggle, or when I inadvertently say something like "lift your heel to your nose" instead of "toes to your nose," I will laugh and say, "Did you hear what I just said?" And everyone will laugh. I want to model to my students to be kind toward themselves—to have fun, lighten up, and not take themselves so *seriously*. It's okay not to execute everything perfectly every time, just to roll with the fumbles, have patience, and enjoy the practice. The same thing applies in our daily life.

Here are some common phrases people use frequently. The phrases in the column on the right are of a higher vibration than those on the left.

Higher-vibrational speech

Lower Vibration	*Higher Vibration*
I have to.	I want to.
I'm caught in a mess.	I intend to find a solution.
I wish I didn't have to go.	I'm choosing to go.
I'm an idiot.	I accept my silly actions.
I'm worried.	I trust.
No problem.	Yes!
You don't make sense.	I intend to understand.
He really set me off.	I was triggered.
I don't want it.	No thank you.
This is stupid.	This doesn't feel right for me.
He's so obnoxious!	I don't resonate with his behavior and the way he expresses.
Things suck here.	I'm being pulled in a new direction.

You make me so angry!	I'm angry right now. I would feel more comfortable if you could please . . .
He is so angry with me.	He is angry.
They rejected me.	My energy is meant to be somewhere else.
I have bad luck.	Circumstances change.
You can't win.	Things work out.
You poor thing.	I trust and know you will be okay.
I can't afford that.	I am not interested in making that purchase.

I remember asking someone, "How are you?" She responded in a spunky tone, "I'm so great I can't stand it!" It caught me off guard because it wasn't the usual "I'm fine, thank you." I laughed all the way into the gym.

Joy is a big part of the language of our heart. Share your funny stories with others, and you will not only be raising your own vibration but also be adding the wonderful high vibration of jubilation to our earth!

There are many layers to learning encouraging and supportive language. I've had to learn how to love myself unconditionally, and I'm still learning. As humans on earth, our learning is infinite and happens gradually, in stages. It's as if we were learning a new language, like Spanish or Arabic or Chinese, for the first time, but this language is the language of the heart.

Take-Away Exercises: Effective Communication Skills

Visualization to Gain Clarity about a Conflict

Give yourself time to meditate and get in touch with your emotions. Sit in your sacred space, close your eyes, breathe deeply, and relax. Visualize that you are connecting with your higher wisdom and with the Divine. Bring the divine love energy into you. Say silently, "My intention is to raise my frequency and connect with the Divine. I intend to align myself to the highest frequency of unconditional love." Place your hands on your heart. Ask your heart, "How am I feeling about this current situation?" "What does my heart need?" Ask your higher self, "Why did this situation bother me so much?" "What needs to be healed within me?" "What am I meant to learn from the situation?" "How did my energy participate in the outcome?" "What is the higher meaning behind this conflict?" "What is the most loving action for me?" "Is communication necessary at this time?" "Is there anything I need to apologize for?" "If so, what is the best way to communicate?" "Am I best served by parting ways now in love and peace?" Trust your intuition, trust what you sense, and stay connected to love. If separating your energy brings up concerns and worries, process them.

Each day is a new day. Nothing is permanent. Stay open for a miracle. Say, "If it feels right someday, I'm open for a loving heart connection; until then, love, wellness, and peace for all parties involved. I intend to view the situation from a connection to unconditional love. I know that I will always be okay and that everything is in divine order."

Exercise for Capturing Your Heart-Touching Moments

Find a jar or vase in your home and put it in a special place. Each time you have a heartfelt moment, take out a piece of colorful paper and write a short description of that moment, expressing how it made you feel. Fold up the paper and put it inside the jar or vase. Continue doing this throughout the year. As frequently as you would like, empty out the jar or vase and read them.

6

STEPPING INTO YOUR SOVEREIGNTY: THE AUTHENTIC YOU

If you have read this far, you've gone through a lot of clearing out! As I take a big breath with you, I understand—it wasn't always easy! You may be wondering, "How did I get here?" And I know you don't ever want to go back, because it feels so good to live life more lightly. All that inner work that you're doing is not only for yourself. It's actually a very selfless act because it uplifts the entire universe. As you raise your own vibration by increasing your joy, empowerment, and inner peace, your higher vibration of light and love raises the level of consciousness. Your frequency creates a ripple effect in your home, your town, and beyond, which affects the entire earth. Who knows where the ripple stops? Personally, I think it keeps right on rolling, to the edge of the solar system, the star cluster, the galaxy, and on and on forever. You are providing a service to your community. You are caring about your emotional footprint as well as your carbon footprint in the environment—another aspect of socially responsible living. You understand that all of your thoughts, words, feelings and emotions create your vibration. You are being the energy you wish to see in the world. You have awakened to your divine self. Our greatest gift to humanity is the healing of ourselves. You understand that everything is energy, and you have transformed yourself into a beacon of light responding to life from a place of power and freedom.

This is just the beginning! It's only going to get better as we continue evolving. New inventions are making their way out to the masses; new ways of living and doing things are cropping up in many grassroots organizations internationally.

I am deeply grateful to you. Thank you for having the courage and inner strength and trust in your inner guidance! You transmuted your disappointments, fears, and sadness into love. You are amazing! It's now time to appreciate who you are, how much you have grown, and where you are headed. Say, "I'm so grateful for the light that I hold today. I intend to stay connected to the higher frequencies of love and light and to ground that light within and around me. Thank you to the Divine for all the help along the way. Today I show loyalty to myself with my kind thoughts toward all parts of me, including my body, mind, emotions, personality, and spirit. I TRUST my infinite abilities as a co-creator of the universe. I am love. I am aware of my codes of infinite power within. Every part of my being is filled with love and light. I connect with it. I feel it. I float upon the earth, expanding my bright light, trusting that miracles and magic abound!"

Your Red-Carpet Walk

I've mentioned this before: *our consciousness creates our reality,* from the inside out. To be able to create the world we want, we must be able to see it first. Let's plant some seeds together and create the most loving, unified, and peaceful world we can imagine. This reality is a mirror of our true essence. We all are birthing this new consciousness together. In this world, you thrive in your own reality, committed to living and being your truth, your divinity. If you lived ONLY in a *love and light* consciousness, as a fully empowering spiritual being connected to the Divine and in your wholeness, what would you be creating here on earth? How would you be expressing yourself? How would you perceive yourself?

Imagine that you are on your own red carpet right now! You are plugged into the channel of unconditional love, light, and unity consciousness. With each step you take, you are seeing manifestations of every wish and dream you have ever had. It's powerful, and it feels so good to finally be totally living and being an expression of your heart in all ways. This is all new to you, and your mind is trying to put it in perspective. But you can't, because it's as if you had entered a new world, a new dimension. With this new view, everything feels lighter, brighter, and more alive. You have really lightened up on yourself, and you feel more relaxed. You are now living the life you always imagined. The peace inside you is like no other feeling you have ever experienced. It is so profound and immeasurable, you're wondering, "Who am I? *Where* am I?" But quickly you intuitively know that you peeled off the old you and amplified and expanded into your true essence. You have never felt this good before; natural and comfortable in your body on earth. With the expansion of your consciousness, your body feels more energized. Your heart is singing, and your spirit is dancing as you accept this new space as your reality. Every day, in this reality, you easily tap into and experience spiritual love from inside you. You have a strong connection with yourself, which is your source of love.

For a split second, you wonder, *"Will this last? Am I dreaming?"* And quickly you drop that thought, knowing that was a tiny tendril of fear left over from your past. With a pair of imaginary scissors, you cut the tendril and watch it fall to the ground, knowing that was the last vestige from the old you. With glee, you look up at the sky with your arms outstretched and your heart wide open, tears welling up in your eyes, and you shout out from the depths of you, *"Thank you! I know I must have been difficult, God; I'm sorry, but thank you for never giving up on me. Thank you for all the support and help you gave me along the way. Thank you for the big push and all the tiny little pushes. I'm so GRATEFUL you didn't give up on me. There were times I didn't think I would make it—or that I even wanted to. I had many doubts and insecurities, so many fears, so much pain, sadness, disappointment, loneliness, and struggle. I don't know how I got here, but I don't ever want to go back. I did it! I made it!"* Tears of gratitude are falling down your face. All your pain is gone. You walked through an inner doorway—a doorway to freedom. This freedom is you.

It feels so good. The air feels fresher. Nature has a new vibrancy with richer and more beautiful, more magical hues. You feel a stronger connection to animals; you can talk to them and feel them more than ever. A dragonfly comes out of nowhere and lands on your hand, as if to give you a special message. You look up the meaning and realize that the universe wanted you to know that you're a reflector of light. *Beautiful confirmation,* you think to yourself. Owls speak to you, sharing their wisdom and reflecting back yours. You say out loud, "I love this new world, this new land. I feel that I'm connected to everything. I love this new human." Your heart and every part of your being is filled up with love and appreciation for the earth, for Mother Gaia. From the depth of your being, you feel connected to this earth like never before. You shout out, "I love you, Gaia; you are always welcome in my energy field." You walk upon the earth with childlike curiosity, with a pure heart, yet filled with wisdom and a newfound love for all existence. Your heart whispers, *"And it's only going to get better."* Finally, your heart is smiling. Your heart is healed, and your mind is at peace. You've waited your whole life to feel this way. Intuitively, you always knew that it truly is all about inner peace, unconditional love, and inner acceptance. This is what you feel now. This is your initiation into this new doorway.

You know that millions of people have entered through this doorway and are experiencing life in a similar way. This door is wide open to more people who also are headed in this direction. With a smile on your face, you feel your body relax, knowing that this is your new earth, your new way of living. There is so much to learn, your mind is open. In this new space you're in, you feel free. You have never felt so authentic and passionate about life.

You skip through your house with joy and gratitude pouring out of your heart. You raise your hand up in the air to high-five your angels and all the unseen loving help and say, "*We did it! Thank you!*"

So . . . here we are. Now what? You're still on earth, maintaining a human body—brushing your teeth, washing your hair, exercising, and paying bills, but living with new beliefs and perceptions.

You think to yourself, "I had no idea it could be this good." In your daily life, you notice that you're bumping into people you don't resonate with from time to time. But the difference is, now you aren't personalizing or attaching to the energy. The energy slides off you. You continue on your way without any judgment and with reverence for everyone. You have the understanding that it's all about choice—choosing a frequency, like choosing a note on a piano. There is only acceptance and reverence toward everyone's unique divine signature. You and others playing similar notes gravitate together as friends, romantic partners, business associates, small communities.

Seeing the humor in life comes naturally to you, and you find that you're giggling more often and spending more time playing with greater abandon. More and more, you allow your true essence and silliness to be seen.

You feel that you are aligned with the highest path for yourself, and you move gracefully with the gentle prodding of your intuition. You allow yourself to flow at the perfect pace, connected to the Divine and moving in the direction of your heart. You have easy access to insight, wisdom, and divine truth within you. Abundance permeates every cell in your body. It is part of your energy as a divine being. It is natural to live in the flow, with ease. The synchronicities in life are abounding. With appreciation you watch the unfolding and perfection of information coming to you at the perfect time. You focus on the specific areas of how you would like to share yourself. It's normal to invest in yourself by spending time enlarging your vision, gathering knowledge, and exerting your energy on positive, authentic activities and creating action plans for your endeavors. Living in this expanded consciousness, you truly live in infinite potential. You use your energy in the highest way possible to help others, by sending positive thoughts and good images—regularly sending them your energy of love and happiness, even to a stranger standing in front of you in the grocery line. You are living in unity consciousness and holding that frequency in your being. This beautiful new light and love energy is assisting with the manifestation of all your heart-centered projects. It's uncanny how quickly things are manifesting around you. You have steadfast belief in yourself and are focused on doing the things that you came to earth to do. All the fear is behind you. You are ready to bring forth your creations.

Your ego is still intact, just more balanced. You are confident yet humble. It feels as if an upgraded operating system is running the show, as if a higher-powered engine is running your human machine. You are not controlled by your emotions anymore. You are equipped with tools that help you realign more quickly and easily into your empowerment. Connections with people are made in perfect timing for projects to come to fruition, for heart connections to be made, and for learning and expansion.

In this world, there are many advances in consciousness. Intuition and telepathy are used and trusted just as frequently as hearing and sight. Your world has expanded with many like-minded people. You have heard of people being able to do remote viewing and even teleport themselves.

You graciously accept the freedom that is bestowed on your sovereignty. A surge of joy flows through you as you find yourself rejoicing and laughing frequently. You feel only unconditional love and support for who you are on the inside. You are free to be happy with who you are, whether you are single, short, old and wrinkled, a woman, divorced, Jewish, Christian, college educated or street smart, a vegan, an organic farmer, or a "tree hugger." You are aware that you have healthier beliefs now that are congruent with your true identity as a loving, spiritual being. You know that you are lovable and that the entire universe is set up for you to be an expression of your divine nature. With this belief, you are relaxed and peaceful. It's as if the fog had disappeared and suddenly, you see things more clearly.

In this reality, you *know* that you are loved so deeply, respected so much, that you wouldn't even consider being anyone other than yourself. There is no racism, sexism, ageism, or egotism. In this world, you are connected to your truth and values and encouraged by everyone to love and live your true essence! You understand that the most aligned way for you to live is doing what brings you joy and makes you happy. During challenging times, everyone rallies together to love and support you. No one is alone going through difficult times. You are connected to your feelings and are able to express yourself with emotional maturity and responsibility.

Everyone who lives in this reality is kind and peaceful, with a healthy sense of who they are, and encouraged to share that love with everyone and everything. We all have a role and understand and trust that we are needed and valued. You have an understanding that your energy affects the whole. Your actions are mutually beneficial for everyone involved. This is a deep understanding of the interconnectedness of everyone and everything. In this world, there is no jealousy, because everyone has a healthy sense of self-worth. There is no competition, because everyone lives with a belief that there is enough to go around. There is a strong faith in the beautiful orchestration of life. In this world, we take complete responsibility for our thoughts, words, beliefs, and actions. There is no suffering, only beauty, truth, and goodness.

In this world of unconditional love and empowerment, we adopt new thoughts, belief systems, and language based on love, truth, and trust. We believe that every human, animal, and plant is divinely created with a unique signature essence that fits perfectly with the whole universe. Each of us is our own star in our world, on our own specific path. We are able to celebrate and love each other and ourselves and respect our divine, beautiful essence as equals. We live in a space of unconditional love. We use only loving, kind, endearing, and nurturing language. The tone of your voice is loving and genuine, and your body language matches your words. Only optimism lives in your reality.

You live in pure joy as you create your life, share your energy, and work in avenues that fit perfectly with your goals and life purpose.

Everyone acts in an authentic, genuine, honest way. You are focused on all the positive things that are emerging, and are getting involved with the foundations, organizations, and groups that resonate with your heart. You find a tremendous sense of purpose and fulfillment co-creating in a cooperative and respectful manner.

In this world, the focus is on solutions, healthier, authentic ways of living, and the betterment of the whole. People here live in harmony with the land and all the creatures of the land and sea and sky. People are very connected to nature and the rest of the animal kingdom. You are aware of your divine codes of infinite power and magical abilities enabling yourself to live on earth as a fully empowered spirit being.

You live more sustainably, growing your own food, sharing gardens with your neighbors, and contributing to conscious communities. Energy and clean water is free and available to everyone. Every state is filled with city parks that have sustainable food forests free to the public.

There is equality and reverence among all people. Women are recognized as powerful and intelligent creators and equals in the workforce. Women independently make their living and support themselves financially. They are not dependent on a partner to support them. Their pay is equal to a man's, and they have the same ability and opportunities as men to grow into management positions within organizations. There is organized child care within the company structure so that working Moms can visit their younger children and breast-feed their babies during the day.

In romantic relationships, there is equality between partners. Both share in the responsibility of raising the children and maintaining the household. Honesty between couples is the normal way of being. When people are in their sovereignty, they are living in a completely transparent and authentic manner. Couples recognize that communication and connection are a priority, and they seek out professionals, elders, teachers, knowledge, healthy practices, and wisdom to support their union. They recognize their union as a priority.

You automatically look for goodness in people and have a strong sense of community. Your focus is on positive action, and you support organizations and groups that are projecting love and light into the world.

There is little fear and much trust, compassion, love, and discernment—discernment of what is right for each individual, with deep trust in one's inner wisdom. Each person powerfully owns her or his own authority and takes complete responsibility for their dominion. People feel a sense of connection, love, inclusion and feel freedom inside their hearts. You live in a healthy, vibrant manner, and you notice that your body is responding to the respectful way that you treat it. Your body seems to have stopped aging, and you feel younger and stronger and look younger, too. You feel a strong connection with your body and intuitively sense what it needs for nourishment, harmony, healing, and balance.

The more people who hold this in our consciousness with our intention and belief system, the quicker this beautiful way of living comes to fruition as our reality. We begin to live in this world in our hearts, in our homes, in our extended families, with our friends, and keep expanding outward in our own communities with this intention. Are you on board in this world? How can you be your desired reality now?

YOU are your own architect, creating your life in every moment. At any moment, you can create something new. Your *desire* gently nudges you forward. Picking up momentum, you begin to use your imagination, building a *vision* for your creation. Like a child, you allow yourself to play. Imagine you are outside in the woods, walking in the dark, and you turn on your flashlight. What do you want in your light beam? What do you see? What do you want to create? Why? How is this going to benefit you and others? What is your inspiration? Once you are clear with your intention and mission, you begin drawing the blueprints, placing your ideas and your *plan* on paper and putting all the pieces together. Who else needs to be involved? Whom do you need to interact with and consult? What do you need to do to bring these people together? What foundation work needs to be done first? What is the best location? Who is the target buyer or audience? What, precisely, is your message or product? What benefits does it bring? How do you *feel* bringing forth this creation? How do you share and express your authenticity? How does this empower you and others?

Now, say YES to your desires by taking action on your ideas, one step at a time: do the research, gather data and knowledge, and meditate.

Let go of any attachment and allow life to unfold, trusting the process. I have always found it helpful to ask that I be on my highest path. Continue to receive your own guidance in your meditations, and follow what feels right for you. Life has its own rhythm. Say, "I am open to this creation or something better. I am open to direction for my highest good and the path of easiest flow." You may begin to fret in your mind, saying, "What if it doesn't happen?" When this happens, *welcome in* your fear. Acknowledge it and process it. Stay in the moment and be flexible and unattached to the outcome.

Continue to fuel your creation with positive thoughts, feelings, and love. During the process, we want to match our frequency with that of our desires. This means to look at any programming or beliefs that say, "This is impossible. I can't do this. I don't believe I'm worthy of this success." If you do have these programs running, process them and upgrade to higher-frequency programs. Begin by stating, "I believe in my abilities as my own creator. I trust my abilities. I choose to be positive. I KNOW this is possible. I KNOW this is the way creation works, and everything is energy. My energy creates everything around me. I'm worthy of being this powerful! I own my power."

Your fears are your past. They are finished and not aligned with your rising vibration. Decide what baby steps you can take to move forward. Spend more time using your imagination to see and feel life as the highest and best image possible.

Your Agreements with Yourself and the Universe

As a powerful being, it's up to you to set in motion your agreements living on planet Earth. Yes, you have that power. Actually, our beliefs and actions are expressing what we agree to and don't agree to, *all the time.* **Here are some examples of agreements. They are a combination of personal and universal agreements. Please write down any of them you agree with, and add your own in your journal.**

Personal Agreements
I agree that I'm the creator of my experiences. I agree to be responsible for my thoughts, beliefs, intentions, and communications in all ways. I agree to expand into my infinite self. I agree to heal the parts within me that feel wounded and separate from my true self. I agree to live in a love, light and empowerment cycle. I agree to connect with the frequency of my divine essence and receive all the gifts of my essence. I agree to live consciously in a physical reality. I agree to live in the most harmonious and natural state as a divine being. I agree to be my authentic self. I agree to loving, sincere, and loyal relationships. I agree to a strong connection to myself, and to value myself. I agree to new beliefs and programs that are aligned with pure potential and the highest probability. I agree to inner peace. I agree to be happy. I agree to follow the commitments I make with

others and myself. I agree to be wealthy, to wealth consciousness and equitable distribution of wealth! I agree to be healthy in body, spirit, and mind and to eliminate toxins from my diet. I agree to maintain a strong, flexible, agile, and healthy body throughout my whole life. I agree to staying young physically and keep my original hair color and height. I agree to value my personal happiness. I agree to feel and express respect for all life. I agree to believe in myself. I agree to share my passion in joyful, respectful environments. I agree to know what love really is as a human on earth. I agree to live as a spiritual being in a human form. I agree to follow my heart and live impeccably. I agree to business relations that are honest, respectful, and mutually beneficial. I agree to build a peaceful world and spread love. I agree to openness and adaptability of the mind. I agree to personal abundance. I agree to co-create with kind, genuine, loving, like-minded individuals. I agree to value inner beauty. I agree to be mindful of my carbon footprint as well as my emotional footprint. I agree to help others.

Universal Agreements

I agree to peace in this world, and I agree to support systems that are based on love and peace. I agree to a world that believes in unconditional love and full empowerment for each being. I agree to organic farming and natural foods and products. I agree to a world that cares for the homeless. I agree to a world that cares about healing people. I agree to a health-care system that integrates allopathic care with naturopathic doctors, alternative care, holistic care, integrative care, and energy healing practitioners. I agree to a wellness system that provides free emotional care practices, tools, and healing techniques to everyone in need. I agree to a wellness system that provides free healing centers for people to go to. I agree to positive and uplifting media. I agree to sustainable living and natural energy sources. I agree to equality for all life. I agree to sufficient food, clean water, shelter, health care, and education for all beings. I agree to support companies that bring inspirational, innovative, positive, helpful services and products to our planet and that work harmoniously with nature. I agree to an educational system that empowers students to believe in themselves, use their creativity, and trust their intuition and empowerment and self-love practices. I agree to humane treatment of animals. I agree to a cooperative, honest, and compassionate political system that listens and respects all humanity. I agree to honest, transparent, compassionate business practices and to companies that care about their employees, compensate them well, and offer them growth opportunities. I agree to a world that operates with compassion, respect, and kindness for all. I agree to an infinite reality for all.

When you are done writing your own list, see if there is anything you can do to take action that supports the direction of your agreements.

Trusting and Believing in Who You *Really* Are

A tree doesn't wonder, "Do I look fat? Why do I keep screwing up?" A tree just does its thing beautifully without competing, without personalizing life or wondering whether the other trees will like it. A tree doesn't look to validate its existence from outside itself. We are meant to be here on earth, just like the trees. You deserve to be. You deserve to feel love and joy and experience life as the glorious, divine, magical being that you are and just to do your thing and *be*!

As sovereign beings, we understand that we are the ones who create the life we want with our thoughts and beliefs. I had a dream that helped me understand this concept more clearly. In the dream, I was on a job interview. My new boss hired me but didn't give me any information about my responsibilities, my salary, or *anything*. The only thing I knew was, I was to begin the next day. The intuitive message I received about the dream was, "Why am I not more definite in my life about what will work for me? The message was to use my power and be clearer, even with the details of what is acceptable for me." Notice whether there are any areas in your life where you can be more precise or detailed or can take the reins and lead the way.

Before coming to earth, we make specific agreements about our missions, lessons to learn, and particular experiences. It is up to us to direct our reality for our highest good and the benefit of all. With this precept, you can trust yourself, trust your heart, and trust that when your intentions and actions are aligned with your heart, you are supported. Then, with flexibility, observe the flow of your life. You are not alone. You have beautiful, divine, loving angelic helpers sharing encouraging messages with you. Just as I was finishing this book and gave the first part to my editor, a hummingbird came to me in my dream. I looked up the symbolism of a hummingbird in the book *Animal Speak*, and this is what it said: "The hummingbird is a symbol for accomplishing that which seems impossible." I felt confirmation of all my efforts in creating this book. Pay attention to the intuitive messages you receive.

There is purpose in everything in our lives. If we observe how life presents itself, we can see the direction and flow of the path we are headed on. What is being presented to you? What is supporting your heart's desires?

If life presents you with more time because you have fewer customers, you're out of a job for the moment, and your life is quieter, this may be because your focus is meant to be on yourself. Maybe things are quiet for you to be able to hear your intuition and pay attention to your emotions. Maybe it's time to start something new like a creative project. Maybe it's time to write a book, restructure your business, expand your beliefs and perspectives, open to new opportunities. Or maybe you're in a period of getting to know yourself better, or you are de-cluttering your life. Everything is on purpose, and you may be generating something new or clearing the way for a new beginning. A quieter time in your life does not mean it is a less valuable or less successful time. This time period is important.

It's important to get calm and still so you can connect with your inner essence, listen, discern, process your emotions, and create intentions and focus on your heart's desires. Humans are getting more comfortable with allowing time for quiet contemplation and meditation. We are realizing the value and benefit. It's not such a weird thing just to sit and breathe, or to sit by a lake and just be present. The quiet allows us to connect with our divinity, which is very powerful. The quiet time is helping us learn about BEING. Just being. Are you comfortable with just being with a sense of full presence? Worries and anxiousness can't live in this space of being. It is the conscious space of I AM. I AM is a state of being, knowing that you are connected to all there is. You feel this sense of being when you're taking a walk and you look up at the sky, spending a few moments in awe and connection with the beauty. You feel this when you are in nature, appreciating and losing yourself in love for a tree, a mountain lake, a butterfly, a caterpillar. You feel this when you are in meditation. State your intention: "I'm willing to experience my I AM presence."

I am responsible for creating my happy ending. And it's your time to create yours. Slow down and celebrate yourself regularly, not just on your birthday. You were born as your authentic self, and now you are meant to go back to that being. I want to thank you personally for doing your healing work, for loving yourself and being here on earth now. There is much to learn, for there are many layers to our glorious, multi-dimensional being. I appreciate how everyone offers uniquely valuable pieces to the puzzle. You are a valuable puzzle piece.

Continue to trust your intuition, and live in a way that feels right for you. You have brought through you more love and light, which has increased the totality of love consciousness on our earth. You are placing new higher agreements into consciousness, which are helping change the entire earth of the future. Enjoy your daily ride! You are an infinite, divine, eternal, beautiful, fully empowered being. Namaste!

Take-Away Exercise: Plugging into the Desired Energy

Sit or lie down in a comfortable place. Close your eyes, take several deep abdominal breaths, and relax. Your intention is to align your energy with your desired outcome.

Visualize long, green garden hoses connected to you. Each garden hose represents an area of your life, such as romance, friendships, abundance, money, business relationships, resources, specific opportunities, or career opportunities. Imagine, one by one, connecting each garden hose into like-minded green garden hoses around the globe. You are plugging into your desired energy.

Say, "*I plug into and feel the energy of _____. I intend to be aligned with this similar vibration, for mutual benefit, for my highest good and the highest good of all. I allow the higher levels of love and light to flood into my reality.*"

Feel the energy that each area brings into your life. Imagine the possibilities along with the feelings and emotions that each connection and plug brings.

Keep your focus on your desires, and let go and fully trust.

ABOUT THE AUTHOR

For more than a decade, Laurie has been providing information and tools for others to empower and inspire themselves. She is a speaker, certified life coach, certified yoga instructor, and the published author of *Smile Across Your Heart: The Process of Building Self-Love* an e-book called *The Conscious Breakup Guide: Navigating Through the End of Your Relationship* and *Language of the Heart: Unconditional Love*. Laurie writes a monthly "Ask Laurie" advice column called "Heart to Heart" for the Naples Daily News. To purchase Laurie's books, yoga DVD, life coaching, online classes and other products and services or to sign up for her newsletter, please visit Laurie's web site: **www.SmileAcrossYourHeart.com**

Email: LOTH@SmileAcrossYourHeart.com

www.ingramcontent.com/pod-product-compliance
Lightning Source LLC
Chambersburg PA
CBHW051830090426
42736CB00011B/1731